DISCOVERING
YOUR GIFTS, VISION, AND CALL

DISCOVERING
YOUR GIFTS, VISION, AND CALL

Jacqueline McMakin
and
Rhoda Nary

HarperSanFrancisco
A Division of HarperCollins*Publishers*

This book was previously published as part four in *Doorways to Christian Growth* by Jacqueline McMakin with Rhoda Nary.

Discovering Your Gifts, Vision, and Call. Copyright © 1993 by Jacqueline McMakin. All rights reserved. Printed in the United States of America. No part of this book may be used or reproduced in any manner whatsoever without written permission except in the case of brief quotations embodied in critical articles and reviews. For information address HarperCollins *Publishers*, 10 East 53rd Street, New York, NY 10022.

FIRST EDITION

Library of Congress Cataloging-in-Publication Data
McMakin, Jacqueline.
[Doorways to Christian growth]
    The doorways series / Jacqueline McMakin and Rhoda Nary.—1st ed.
        p. cm.
    Originally published as a single volume in 1984, under the title:
Doorways to Christian growth.
    Includes bibliographical references.
    Contents: [1] Encountering God in the Old Testament—[2] Meeting Jesus in the New Testament—[3] Journeying with the spirit—[4] Discovering your gifts, vision, and call.
    ISBN 0–06–065377–9 (v. 1).—ISBN 0–06–065378–7 (v. 2).—ISBN 0–06–065379–5 (v. 3).—ISBN 0–06–065380–9 (v. 4).
    1. Christian life—1960-   2. God—Biblical teaching.   3. Jesus Christ—Person and offices.   I. Nary, Rhoda.   II. Title.
[BV4501.2.M4358 1993]
248.4—dc20   92–53917
                                                                          CIP

93 94 95 96 97 ❖ HAD 10 9 8 7 6 5 4 3 2 1

This edition is printed on acid-free paper that meets the American National Standards Institute Z39.48 Standard.

CONTENTS

INTRODUCTION

What shall I do with my life?

Personal and societal problems surround us. There are many worthy claims on our time. Committed people want to respond but need focus and direction.

This book is about how to find that focus and direction. From the wisdom of our Christian tradition we learn that God calls us to collaborate in extending God's love. A way to discover the focus for this call is to reflect on God's vision and the piece of that vision that is given to us. To implement vision we are given gifts. Through reflection on our gifts, vision, and call, we find focus and direction for our lives.

To help us do that, this book explores six questions:

1. What are my unique gifts?

2. How can I call forth another's gifts?

3. Which vision is mine to carry?

4. What is God calling me to do?

5. How can I work together with those who share my call?

6. How can the larger community support the callings of its members?

The question form is deliberate. It opens us to the many dimensions of God's guidance that might otherwise be missed. These are not the only questions to ask, but they provide a good start. The order in which they are presented is logical but not necessarily how they occur in our lives. The first four questions form a discernment process that helps us listen to God's call. Session 5 focuses on how to create servant communities through which to carry out our call. Session 6 discusses how a parish or other organization can become a "community of communities" that supports the calls of its members.[1]

Three afflictions plague modern people. Fragmentation scatters our energy. Burnout demoralizes us. And powerlessness causes us to stop before we start.

The concepts and questions in this book teach another way. The best experience from the most vital Christian communities shows us how to focus our energy, nourish our commitment, and activate powerful change for good.

The purpose and spirit of this book are captured in the words of a greeting card sent by one of our participants. They are a good note on which to begin:

A vision without a task
is a dream.
A task without a vision
is a drudgery.
A vision and a task
is the
hope
of the world.[2]

PREFACE TO
THE DOORWAYS SERIES

Two of us were rambling along a trail on a sparkling spring day. One was discouraged, did not know where her life was going. The other felt content and grateful for a time to see what was happening in the woods.

Suddenly we stopped. Across our path lay a branch, broken off and seemingly dead. But there right on that branch burst forth a blossom that beamed at us in greeting.

We looked at each other and smiled. In that flower, God had broken in on us with a message: life can burst forth unexpectedly and bless us with its presence.

This brief story came to mind as we were thinking about the purpose of the four books in the *Doorways* Series. They are for people with hope, energy, and commitment who want reinforcement. They also are for dispirited people who question the direction of their own lives and of society.

The books invite you to taste nourishing spiritual food discovered by people in one particular faith path—the Christian tradition. From the core of this tradition radiates an astounding truth: there is at the heart of the universe a cherishing presence that holds all creation in a loving embrace. To be nurtured by this love is to be infused by fresh life.

In a fast-moving, multifaceted society, people look for anchors to hold them steady. Mobility makes us long for a sense of belonging. Pressing personal and societal needs make us wonder where we fit and how we can contribute.

The *Doorways* Series was written in response to these yearnings. It helps us listen to our own truth and sink our roots in a solid tradition. It takes us on a journey of discovery. Its purpose is to help us grow in spiritual awareness, learn to build community where we are, and be more fully God's person at home, at work, and in the other places where we spend our time.

Underneath our yearnings are profound questions. Each book in the *Doorways* Series focuses on one question most of us ask at one time or another:

✚ Who is God?

✚ Who is Jesus?

✚ How can I nourish my spirit?

✚ What should I do with my life?

To aid you in addressing these questions, this series offers twenty-four dynamic stories, images, and concepts found in the Christian tradition. When you allow all parts of your body, mind, and spirit to engage with these treasures, you will be enlarged, enhanced, empowered.

Included in each book are activities for you, the reader, as well as for a group. Thus, each book can be used as a course. Designed originally by a community of Catholic and Protestant laypeople, the courses include wisdom and practices from each tradition that we have found powerful in our own lives. The courses build on each other, but each can be used on its own.

In their time with Jesus, the disciples had a training experience—living, learning, doing. They moved from being neophytes to well-trained healers and teachers. These courses are designed to replicate this experience of growth for us twentieth-century people, to equip us to live the committed life. Each of the *Doorways* courses presents a different challenge.

Encountering God in the Old Testament provides a way to explore the understandings of God realized by people in the Old Testament. This introductory course is suited to people with no prior experience of faith as well as to longtime churchgoers who are taking another look at the meaning of faith.

Meeting Jesus in the New Testament offers opportunities to learn about the Jesus of history and to make faith decisions today in response to the living presence of the Spirit. It is for those who want to be more than observers of the ministry of Jesus, who want to explore being companions in that work.

Journeying with the Spirit is for those who are committed to the way of Jesus and who would like to strengthen that commitment through experiencing classic resources for growth such as prayer, meditation, healing, and reconciliation.

Discovering Your Gifts, Vision, and Call is for people concerned with the pain and disharmony in the world and who want to help implement God's vision for the world. It offers a discernment process for discovering one's gifts and calling as well as ideas for forming communities to give communal expression to it.

These four courses are progressive in that they build on a deepening relationship with God and provide opportunities to:

✤ *explore* experiences of God;

✤ *decide* about one's relationship to God;

✤ *deepen* those decisions;

✤ *discern* life direction and purpose.

We offer these books to each of you as you seek to find your particular way of making the world a better place. If current environmental degradation teaches anything, it is that every person on Earth must become involved in preserving this precious creation. To build the kind of global resolve necessary will require commitment and stamina, which come from being firmly rooted in sources of spiritual power.

HOW TO USE THIS BOOK
AS A COURSE

This book is designed not only to be read but to be used as a course for individuals and groups. As an individual, you can gain much from "doing" this book in your own way and in your own timing. Adapt the Group Design exercises to yourself and try them out. Do the Individual Work. Perhaps you can find another person with whom to share the course or to discuss some of its aspects. If you are motivated to work alone with the content, honor that instinct and have confidence that your efforts will bear fruit.

Groups that can benefit from the material are existing Bible-study, life-sharing, or task groups who want to grow together, or groups especially convened for the particular training offered through these courses.

✣ How the Material Is Organized ✣

Each book includes an introduction, six sessions, and ideas for further reflection and next steps. Each of the six sessions includes:

✣ Session Text: basic content material on the topic;

✣ Group Design: practical ways for a group to work with the content in the session text;

✣ Individual Work: suggestions on how to apply the content to our own lives as individuals.

✚ Using the Material in Groups ✚

In order to get the most from the course, it is important to do three things:

1. Read and Digest the Text.　Before coming to the first meeting, read the Introduction, How to Use This Book as a Course, and Session 1 text in preparation. To prepare for the second session, read text for Session 2, and so on through the six sessions of the book. It is best to devote most of your time between meetings to the Individual Work related to the preceding session before reading the new session. Leave the new session for the day or so before you meet.

2. Participate in the Group Design.　When people relax and participate in the group activities, much growth occurs. No design is perfect, and no design works equally well for all groups. Don't be bound by these design ideas, but do take time to understand their underlying purpose. If you can accomplish the same goals in other ways, great. You may want to modify the timing on the designs. We estimate that our timing works easily for groups of about twelve people. Smaller groups will have more time; larger groups may have to shorten or omit certain activities.

Each Group Design has several parts that we will look at in detail.

Gathering Time:　The purpose of this is to assemble the group and ready yourselves for the session. Since we have built in ways to share personal information throughout the design, this does not have to be accomplished fully in the gathering time. Ten minutes is usually sufficient. Divide the time equally among all of you and really listen to each person. Resist the temptation to allow more time for this section or to be undisciplined in its use.

Sharing Groups: These are groups of four that you form at the first session. The purpose of these is to share in a small setting what you did with the suggestions for the Individual Work and to support one another as you take the course. These same groups meet at least once during each session. We find there are many benefits when the same group meets consistently. To get to know others in the larger group, there will be activities to do with them in other parts of the session.

Discussion of the Session Text: We have included discussion of the text only occasionally because we felt it useful to give more time to other activities. However, if your group would like to discuss it each time, feel free to do so. Here's a sample discussion question: What learning from the text was most important for you?

Lab Exercise: The purpose of the lab exercise is to enable the group to experience one aspect of the topic and reflect on this experience. The activities in this section vary a great deal. Some are lighthearted, while others are more serious. Participants have found them all to be valuable.

Closing: This time is meant to give people an opportunity to reflect on the session and to have closure. Sometimes we offer a suggestion about how to do this; at other times we leave it to you. Some groups like to vary their closing exercises; others like the consistency of the same ending each time, such as a favorite song or a circle of prayer.

Materials: We suggest that you bring a Bible and a notebook for each session. When additional materials are needed, this is indicated in the design.

Breaks: According to your group's needs, schedule a five- to ten-minute break in the middle of each session. Our estimated timing does not include breaks, so adjust your timing accordingly. Tell people at the beginning of the session when the break will be.

3. Do the Individual Work. This work is designed to be done at home between sessions and is an important part of the course. It is a bridge between sessions and provides ways for you to integrate the content. Our participants find this one of the most worthwhile parts of the experience and urge us to underscore its importance.

The Individual Work usually involves fifteen to thirty minutes of quiet time per day for reading, reflection, and writing your thoughts in a journal, usually a loose-leaf notebook. At the end of each week it is useful to write a one-paragraph summary of what you did, your particular learnings and difficulties, and any questions. This summary can be shared with the group.

We suggest that you devote the quiet times during the first part of your week to the Individual Work and that you use the last few days before your group session to read the new chapter in preparation for the next session.

For the six weeks of the course, budget the time you need to do the Individual Work. It is integral to the course.

✤ What About Leadership? ✤

Don't rely on just one person to make your group thrive. Leadership is needed for two functions: *facilitation* and *organization*. Consider finding two people for each function. Choose these people on the basis of gifts and motivation. Who would really like to do what?

Facilitation: This can be done by the same person or pair each time or rotated so everyone in the group takes a turn. As the group facilitator you will:

✤ read the session text, Group Design, and Individual Work in advance;

✤ gather the necessary materials for the next session;

✤ convene the group at the start of the session;

✤ lead it through the Group Design, keeping to the time you agree on;

✤ close the meeting with a reminder of the time and place of the next session.

There are additional ways you as a facilitator can help the group. You might:

✤ do some background reading.

✤ add your creativity to the Group Design, tailoring it to the needs of the group.

✤ pray for the people in the group.

✤ give examples from your own life to begin sharing times. The way you do this modeling is important. If your example is long, other people's examples will be long. If you share from the heart, others are likely to do the same. By your example you give others freedom to be open. Our participants tell us that when they hear leaders share authentic pains and joys, they feel encouraged to face similar feelings in their own situations.

✤ be attentive to nonverbal communication in the group. As a leader, you can foster an atmosphere of caring, genuineness, and openness through a smile, a word of encouragement, a touch on the arm.

Organization: This, too, can be done by the same person or pair each time, or rotated. To help in this way you can:

✤ publicize the course by placing notices in newsletters, making personal phone calls to invite people to attend, and distributing flyers;

✤ be attentive during the session to people's reactions and lend encouragement to those who need it;

✤ call absent people between times to fill them in on what happened;

✤ see that refreshments are provided, if the group wishes them;

✤ pray for the individuals in the group.

We call the organization people *shepherds* since they look after and care for each person individually, leaving the facilitators free to care about group process and content. After facilitating courses with the assistance of shepherds, we would never be without them. They make a major difference in the quality and depth of a course. Shepherding is a wonderful gift that some people have and enjoy using.

✤ How to Gather a Group ✤

Suppose you would like to gather a group to take a *Doorways* course together. Find another person who will work with you and who has enthusiasm about doing the course. Consider whether to seek church sponsorship. To find people who would like to take the course and to prepare them to participate fully, you can do these things:

1. *Spread the word as widely as possible.*

Start with family, friends, neighbors, members of groups active in the church and community, and newcomers. Try to contact these people personally. Tell them the purposes of the course: to provide spiritual nourishment, to build a caring and supportive group, and to discover which part of God's work we are called to foster. (To become clearer about the purpose for each course, read the introductory material in the beginning of the course.)

People respond to an invitation to join the course for a variety of reasons: some are looking for a sense of belonging; others want purpose or direction in their lives; others are hungry for spiritual nourishment. Find out what people are looking for and then describe how the course addresses their needs.

2. *Be sure to go over procedural matters such as the dates, time, and place for the course.*

If possible, hold the course in a comfortable, home-like atmosphere.

Explain that the course depends on the commitment of all the members to come regularly, to be on time, to do the Individual Work, and to let someone know if they will be absent so they can be brought up-to-date before the next session.

3. *Let people know that the method used will be experiential learning.*

This style depends on the participation of each person and not on the expertise of a leader. Participants learn by doing. You each proceed at your own pace and in your own way. Some people will have important insights during the group meetings; others may have them at home; others may see results from the course only after it has ended.

This style of learning contrasts with traditional ways of teaching in which someone in authority (a theologian, pastor, or teacher) offers content to a learner, whose main job is to assimilate and apply it. Some people may expect a traditional approach and ask questions such as "Who's teaching the course? Who's the leader?" Sometimes we offer this explanation: The traditional approach is useful for imparting doctrine (the wisdom and teachings of the church throughout history). Experiential learning enables us to examine some of those doctrines and make them a living part of our lives. The facilitators of the course are learners with all the others who take it.

4.   *Pray together for the group.*

That can make the difference between gratitude and frustration in gathering a group. When you pray, you may be given inspiration about new people to contact or new ways to do it.

5.   *Determine the size and makeup of the group.*

The course works well with groups numbering from ten to twenty, people of all ages, clergy and laity, men and women.

What Are My Unique Gifts?

"I love what I do," says Samuel Hale, founder of International Resources Group in Washington, D.C., and a member of the Society of Friends. His company plants trees in deforested regions around the world and participates in a variety of other environmental projects. "Not only do I get to do things I enjoy—travel, develop projects, communicate across cultures—I feel I'm contributing something worthwhile to society."

The world would be wonderful if it were filled with people who, like Sandy Hale, use their gifts to embody God's compassion. What follows are key biblical teachings on gifts and then some pointers on how to identify and cultivate your own gifts.

Jesus prepared his disciples to be on their own after his death. They had learned much about what the world would look like if God's ways were to prevail. Jesus had told many "realm of God" parables, stories designed to cause his followers to think for themselves and make hard choices. Then he told one that, on the surface, seemed cruel.

The realm of God, said Jesus, is like a man going on a journey who called together his servants and entrusted his property to them. To one he gave five talents (weights used as currency), to another two, and to a third one. Then he set out. The first man traded his share and doubled his wealth. The second did likewise. But the third buried his talent. When the master returned, he wanted a report. The first two proudly produced the additional talents, which pleased the master greatly. The third said that because he was afraid of the master, he hid his share. And so he had only one talent to give back.

At this, the master raged: "You wicked and lazy servant!" Seizing the one talent, he gave it to the man who had five, and ordered the "one talent man" thrown out into "the dark, where there will be weeping and grinding of teeth" (Matt. 25:14–30, JB).

Why did Jesus tell such a harsh story? To drive home his point that using gifts is crucial to living life fully. In fact, Jesus deemed it a matter of life and death. He presented choices. If you use the gifts that have been given to you, they will grow, and you will flourish. If you hide them in fear, they cannot grow, and you will be consumed by anger and frustration.

Jungian therapist Marie von Franz explains how this happens:

> People get absolutely intolerable when they have a creative idea in their womb and can't bring it out. They're neurotic, aggressive, irritable, and depressed.[1]

Our God-given gifts are meant to be used fully, or we and others suffer tremendous loss. The discovery and exercise of gifts is not an optional luxury but is crucial to our being full persons of God at work, at home, and everywhere. We cannot love others fully until we love who we are and what we are doing—in other words, until we are exercising our gift, whatever it is. Says nationally syndicated radio and television psychotherapist David Viscott:

> I only know one truth: Whatever you love, do that. If you're not doing what you love, you're not going to do anything well.[2]

This point is borne out by many people who, when asked what they want most from what they do, answer, "The chance to be creative." Using gifts is crucial to doing our best at work.

Excellent work is a foundation of a healthy society. In analyzing how to invigorate American life, Robert Bellah and his colleagues concluded in *Habits of the Heart*:

Work that is intrinsically interesting and valuable is one of the central requirements for a revitalized social ecology.[3]

As Paul went about encouraging the early Christians, he wrote about gifts in his letters. His message to the Ephesians (Eph. 4:11–16) was summarized by Pat Davis, one of our early associates, in this way:

Every person called by Jesus Christ into his body
is given a gift
to use
on behalf of the whole body!

"In other words, everyone is gifted!" Pat concluded. "You can be what you were intended to be and do what you were created to do."

Elsewhere, in a wonderful image, Paul advised young Timothy "to fan into a flame the gift that God gave you"—(2 Tim. 1:6, JB). So important did Paul think this was that he urged us to focus on our gifts, develop them, and offer them with full enthusiasm.

If our gift is preaching, let us preach to the limit of our vision. If it is serving others let us concentrate on our service; if it is teaching let us give all we have to our teaching; and if our gift be the stimulating of the faith of others let us set ourselves to it. (Rom. 12:6–8, Phillips)

The specific gifts that Paul mentions here are particularly suited to faith settings. His list is only the beginning. The variety of gifts we have been given is really endless.

We use the term *gift* broadly. Whether you are starting out, retired, or in the middle of your most productive years, you are created with unique talents, characteristics, propensities, and capacities. On top of that, you have accumulated experiences. All of these are gifts when used for creative purposes. When you use them to build a home or business, to till the land or fashion a garment, you feel as if all of you is being used. You can then throw yourself into what you do and have a good time doing it.

Knowing what your gifts are and having the courage to use them is not always easy. The double messages given to us all through life make it tough to recognize and be confident about our giftedness. "You're great!" we heard when we first stumbled onto the stage. But if we said, "Wasn't I great!" we were told not to brag. "You have a talent for painting," encouraged our father. "But you're not doing it right," said our teacher.

Opposing messages dampen creativity. It then becomes natural to bury that desire to build, to squeal and yell, to get messy and experiment, to explore and wander. Instead, we sit still, do what we are told, bend ourselves to other peoples' agendas, or escape into television.

Understanding what has been given us and how we can put these gifts to work is a fundamental key to unlocking our potential. To identify your gifts, follow these steps.

First, *recognize that this is a good and valuable thing to do* that has deep spiritual roots in our tradition.

Second, *ask God for guidance*. You are created in God's image. Reflect on what that means specifically.

Third, *ask these questions:*

✤ What is it I love to do?

✤ What types of things express the real me?

✤ What do I think I am really good at doing or being?

✤ What makes me feel satisfied or proud?

✤ What comes out of my center?

If these questions throw you, give yourself time to identify what really delights *you*, makes *you* feel fully alive.

Mexican attorney Pepe Visoso felt dissatisfied with his work as a trial lawyer. Reflection on the above questions resulted in valuable discoveries.

> Although I knew I had a good legal mind, I realized that what I really loved was not winning in court, but rather persuading people to settle outside of court. I discovered I am good at bringing people to discussion, giving them confidence that they can come to agreement. I love coming up with a decision that is good for all parties, not just those paying my fee.

These insights led Pepe to refocus his legal practice in order to concentrate on mediation.

What is a gift for one may not be for another. At first glance, losing a leg to cancer would not be considered a gift. Yet for Ted Kennedy, Jr., it became the qualifying and motivating experience he offers in work with other disabled people. Thus, in his case, what was a tragedy has become a gift.

Families, businesses, schools, and churches are in a unique position to call forth peoples' gifts, and when they do, good things happen.

The Church of the Saviour in Washington, D.C., is organized around the gifts and vision of its people. It defines itself as a gift-evoking and gift-bearing community. It offers encouragement, instruction, and "friendly open space," as priest-psychologist Henri Nouwen puts it, to help people identify their gifts and calling. It encourages those with similar callings to gather for support and common work. Each group creates ways to grow together spiritually, to care about one another, and to implement their calling. Groups are as diverse as people's interests. Called "mission groups," they have been organized to care for neglected children in the city, to create affordable housing, to provide retreats for rest and reflection, and to support people in public-policy work.

Founding minister Gordon Cosby ties together the importance of gifts for ourselves and society:

> I think all of us had best find out what we really want to do and start doing it with whatever it involves. If you have to give up your responsibility, give it up; if the Church goes to pieces, so be it. But we've got to find what we want to do, *really*, because nothing else is going to help anybody.[4]

This has a ripple effect whenever it happens. Cosby also writes:

> When you have the time of your life doing what you're doing, this has a way of calling forth the deeps of another person. . . . You are not talking about "good news"; you *are* "good news." You are the embodiment of the freedom of the new humanity.[5]

Cosby challenges us to help one another discover what we really want to be and do. This does not necessarily mean that we leave our job or location. What it does entail is a change of perspective and attitude, allowing what delights and energizes us to blossom in whatever we do. The following exercises and sessions focus on ways to do this.

GROUP DESIGN

Purpose: To identify some of our individual gifts and to reflect on scriptural passages related to gifts.

Materials: 8½ x 11 unlined scrap paper and thin marking pens.

A. Gathering Time, Large Group (*twenty minutes*)

Describe either a gift given or received that had importance for you. For example, one person in our group said, "What comes immediately to my mind was the truckload of manure the kids and I gave my husband one year for his birthday. He loves to garden, so we borrowed a truck, filled it, and the kids decorated it with clanging cans and streamers and drove down the driveway yelling 'Happy Birthday' at the top of their lungs."

B. Looking at My Gifts, Individuals and Pairs (*twenty minutes*)

1. Each person take a sheet of paper and some marking pens, draw a picture of yourself complete with head, body, heart, hands, feet, etc. Then add, in a word, what you love doing with each part of yourself. For example, by your feet you might put "hiking and skiing," by your hands, "carpentry work." Then above the figure draw circles representing the places in which you offer yourself— i.e., family, friends, church, self, work, local municipality. Then consider this question: If you had enough time and could do anything, give anything, or be anything in one of these places, what would you like to give, be, or do, and in which place? When you have answered, draw a circle around one thing you love doing and connect it with the circled place (family, friends, etc.) where you most want to use it now.

2. When all have finished, each one choose a person you know least well in the group and share some of what you drew.

C. Sharing Groups (*twenty minutes*)

Each pair from the previous exercise choose another pair and continue to share drawings. The foursomes you form will then become your sharing groups for subsequent sessions. Before concluding this time, jot down the names and phone numbers of those in your foursome.

D. Building a Group Theology of Gifts, Small Groups and Large Groups (*fifty minutes*)

1.   Divide the group into six small groups. Give each group one of these Scripture passages for study: 2 Tim. 1:6–7; Rom. 12:4–8; 1 Cor. 12:1–11; 1 Cor. 12:27–30; Eph. 4:11–16; Matt. 25:14–30. Each group move to separate corners of the room or to separate rooms for study.

2.   Each small group read your Scripture passage aloud. Spend a few minutes in silent reflection on what in that Scripture seems important to you. When all are ready, share your insights. Allow about fifteen minutes for this.

3.   Reconvene in the large group. Informally sum up the passage you studied and one or two insights that occurred in each group. At the end of the sharing, one or two people might summarize the total group's theology of gifts. Use about twenty-five minutes for this part.

E. Closing, Large Group (*ten minutes*)

Choose from the following suggestions as appropriate for your group.

1.   Evaluate this session. (In a few words, what was helpful? What was not helpful?) Quickly share any ideas for improvement for next session.

2.   Sing.

3.   Pray (give thanks for one gift mentioned for each individual in the group—e.g., "Thanks for Dick's humor").

4.   Discuss details of next session if necessary (time, place, leadership responsibility).

INDIVIDUAL WORK

Purpose: To reflect further on scriptural understandings of gifts and to continue work on identifying our own gifts.

1.   Read and meditate daily on 1 Cor. 12:1–11, an overview of spiritual gifts with emphasis on their unitive spirit. Other references used during the session are Matt. 25:14–30; Eph. 4:11–16; Rom. 12:4–8; 2 Tim. 1:6–7; 1 Cor. 12:27–30. Ponder and pray, using any or all of these passages. Note what comes alive or what seems particularly relevant to your situation.

2.   Identifying your gifts: For this we use an exercise devised by Bernard Haldane, an employment consultant. The purpose is to focus on those things you really love to do; this is one way of discerning your gifts.

   a. Make a list of good experiences you have had in your life. Divide your life into four quarters (if you are forty, you will have four periods of ten years each). For each quarter, list five experiences, using this definition of the term:

   ✤ something you enjoyed doing;

   ✤ something you felt you did well;

   ✤ something that made you feel satisfied or proud.

   You can list any sort of thing: learning to whistle, building a tree house, creating an event, taking a trip, learning a new skill. Make sure they are things that have meaning for you personally. It is not important that others recognized their value.

Many people groan when they contemplate doing this. We have been taught to be modest and to hide what gives us delight. Some people think they don't have many good things in their lives. Be patient and work on your list in odd moments throughout the week while driving or working around the house. Things will occur to you.

Note: Don't try to do the whole list at one sitting or leave it to the last minute. It takes time.

b. Go over your list and choose three good experiences you would like to talk about with others.

c. *Please bring your list to the next session.*

3. At the end of the week, summarize in writing what you did with this session in preparation for the next session.

SESSION 2

How Can I Call Forth Another's Gifts?

Occasionally a baby is born with no assistance other than from its mother. Usually, however, some kind of help—from a doctor, midwife, husband, friend—is not only helpful but necessary.

So it is with our gifts. If they are to emerge, develop, mature, and be put to good use, other people's help can make all the difference. In writing about these helpers, Elizabeth O'Connor resurrected the term *patron*, a word with rich associations.[1]

We are familiar with the patroning work of churches and individuals who *discovered*, *affirmed*, and *found outlets* for the gifts of Renaissance artists and Baroque musicians. Indeed, the survival of some of these artists and musicians depended on the generosity and ingenuity of their patrons. Without their patrons' sponsorship, many of these creative people would have had to quit artistic pursuits for more practical and lucrative work.

Elizabeth O'Connor suggests that we all need patrons if our gifts are to flourish. This session looks at how patrons empower us and offers suggestions about how to find patroning for ourselves and offer it to others.

The Christian tradition is replete with examples of people helping one another offer their gifts. Jesus cared about the development of his followers. He took them aside to give coaching, encouragement, a probing question, a listening ear. When the first tiny Christian communities sprang into being in Jerusalem, Ephesus, and Philippi, one could not become a full-fledged member until meeting with someone new to the church and encouraging them in their gift of faith. Later, in monastic communities, novice directors looked after the newcomers, shepherding their spiritual development.

Pope Julian asked Michelangelo to paint the Sistine Chapel. Believing in the gifted artist, he gave him opportunities to work, showed his paintings, helped find commissions. For Michelangelo, Pope Julian was a patron.

Not only is patroning the affirmation of our gifts, it also *helps us uncover our gifts*. Someone may say, "I'd love to use my gifts, but I don't know what they are. I don't think I have any gifts." That is a patroning moment, the opportunity for a patron to make a real difference.

There are many reasons why some people's first reaction to "What are your gifts?" is "I don't have any." Negative messages take their toll. In a study of innovation potential, which involves creative use of gifts, George Ainsworth-Land, philosopher and consultant, found this:

> At age five, 98% were judged to have innovative potential; by age ten the percentage had dropped to 30%; and by 15 to 12%. . . . By and large, organizations today still reward emulation rather than innovation. As a result by age 30 only 2% of the subjects in the study are judged to have high innovative potential. Perhaps not surprisingly, the percentage begins to rise significantly at around retirement age.[2]

It is not that people lack gifts. But often these gifts remain hidden or have been dampened by poor parenting, schooling, or work experiences. Patrons can help strip away those negative influences and recognize in us treasures we have lost the ability to see. The biblical story of Lazarus, when considered metaphorically, helps us understand how to spring loose from these negative influences.

A man died and, according to custom, was wrapped in funeral clothes and placed in a tomb. His distraught sisters sent a message to their friend Jesus, the itinerant healer, and pleaded for him to work a miracle. "He is only sleeping," Jesus said to his disciples. When Jesus arrived at the man's tomb, he called, "Lazarus, here! Come out!" To everyone's amazement, "The dead man came out, his feet and hands bound with bands of stuff and a cloth around his face." To the anxious onlookers, Jesus said, "Unbind him, let him go free" (John 11:1–44, JB).

Like Lazarus, our vital, gifted selves need unwrapping from the influences that have deadened us. And notice, the friends of Lazarus were needed to do the unbinding. Only with help was Lazarus able to emerge.

We bring forth one another's fullness when we focus on the good in people rather than their shortcomings. Bruce Larson, author and pastor, remembers when he could think of his son, during the "terrible twos," only as "Mr. Trouble." How damaging he realized that was. So, in his mind's eye, he named his little toddler, "Mr. Wonderful." Everything changed. Bruce relaxed and enjoyed his son, who, in turn, responded more positively.

This is what being a patron is all about—seeing one another as wonderful, full of wonder and untapped potential waiting to be coaxed into existence. When we do this, we call forth one another's uniqueness. Then each of us has more to bring to the job, the family, the community, the church.

What does a patron do? We've already noted what Renaissance and Baroque patrons did. Think of those teachers, parents, or colleagues who have particularly *encouraged you, believed in you, called you forth*. They did it in dozens of ways—through a look, a smile, a pat on the back, lending you a book, asking for your help.

A patron helps us *identify the gifts we have by naming them or helping us name them, perhaps in a way that is particularly fitting or evocative*. This happens in our groups when participants speak with one another about things they do well and enjoy doing. The others act as listeners or patrons. Their task is to hear carefully the person's description of delightful, exciting, or motivating experiences and then to hazard a guess as to what gifts were used by the person in those experiences. Finally, the person is invited to confirm or modify the names put forward.

When Jack described how he, as a city boy, had gone far from home to work on a farm, and how he was one of the first in his college to work out a foreign study experience, his patron delighted him by saying, "You're a pioneer!" One of our partners, Lois Donnelly, described in colorful detail how she had made special outfits for herself and her daughters to welcome her husband home from his military tour in Okinawa: "Tom had sent us some red raw silk from Japan which I used. Then I made red and white pom-poms that we waved in the air as the ship came into view. There were fifteen hundred Marines madly waving. Tom claimed he saw us first. Even as I think back on it now, tears come. It was one of the most moving moments of my life." Then she spoke about an anniversary party she arranged for family and friends with a "make your own wild ice cream concoction" finale. When her patron said, "You're an occasion maker," she replied, "Yes, I love doing that."

A patron is concerned with *understanding and encouraging the uniqueness of the other person's gifts*. For example, in discussing the gift of listening, one of our groups realized there are different types of listening gifts. Some people listen best in situations in which a person needs support or encouragement to hang on in a difficult situation. The group described this as a hand-holding kind of listening or supporting. Others feel their listening gifts are best used in enabling persons to move and change. The group kiddingly called this a "shove-off-the dock" or motivating listening. Clearly, good listening can involve both supporting and motivating, but some people are better at one than the other. Perhaps in finding outlets for their gifts, persons who are good at offering support might consider working with the bereaved, whereas those who are motivators might better counsel people in transition.

A patron can *help you sort through which gifts you want to use.* A group of her friends gathered around Meg Tucillo and listened to her describe some of her good experiences; they then named gifts they saw in her.

"You're a nurturing person. You always care about me in tough times," said one man. Meg replied listlessly, "Yes, I guess so."

"You've always fixed such great food for our gatherings; you have the gift of cooking, for sure."

"I know," said Meg. "That's true." But there was no life in her answer.

Finally one person asked, "Meg, tell us why you listed ice skating. What was that all about?"

Immediately, Meg lit up. "Oh, that was when I was a teenager in New Jersey. My dad would flood the backyard, which then froze over, and we had our own skating rink. My sister and I dressed up like skating stars—in short skirts and white stockings. We looked terrific!" Meg was more animated. "Dad rigged up lights. At night, with the lights on, we'd get the neighbor kids over and have a skating show. It was fabulous!"

We caught her enthusiasm. "I know," said one person. "You're a ham!"

"You like to be behind lights. You've got the gift of show biz!"

"Yes, I do!" exclaimed Meg, beaming. "Yes, I love being out there, acting, making a fool of myself, performing. I love it."

Meg was burned out using her cooking and nurturing gifts. Hamming it up was a gift she was eager to use. That winter she starred in her church's anniversary spoof called "Flounder!"

The first friends who spoke to Meg had identified gifts she was tired of using, or gifts they wanted her to use. It was the last person who helped Meg see which gift would add freshness to her life.

A patron can *suggest and provide ways for different gifts to work together*. Observing *campesinos* who want to continue to farm as well as local business people who want to help that happen, Lorenzo Servitje founded the Mexican Rural Development Foundation. Its board obtains funds for credit. Then local businesspeople vouch for the farmers at the bank, who can thus get financing for their projects. The different gifts of businesspeople, farmers, and board members combine to revitalize neighborhoods.

Pointing to *how gifts combine within a person* is another way a patron works. One of our artistic participants was dividing her time between painting, volunteer work with the elderly, and clerking in a store to earn some money. Her patron named a way to combine her gifts: art therapy for the elderly.

If you walk into our local beauty shop, you will notice that a patron has been at work. On the walls are displayed artist Pat Olson's beautiful watercolor paintings. They have been hung there by shop owners Evelyn and Ken Bellas. In this way, they *introduce Pat Olson's work to other people*.

Another important function of a patron is expressed by a sculptor we know. He says that having friends who are *consumers* of his creations—that is, who use his pieces or find uses for them—is vital to the exercise of his gift.

The work of discovering and using gifts is delightful, but it also can create problems, especially if your gifts are different from the gifts of those around you. The high schooler who devotes time to piano study may be seen as "weird," while another involved in football practice is considered a "hero." If you excel at swimming and win all the prizes, others can be envious. To develop a gift may mean to move out from the crowd, and that can be difficult. Helping young people face these problems, Wally Gibbs, youth minister in New Rochelle, New York, had a vivid way of *reassuring* them:

If you don't step on someone's toes once in a while,
chances are you're not moving!

No one wants to cause misunderstanding or conflict, but sometimes these are a part of growth. A patron can *help another live with,
learn from, and move through these kinds of negative reactions*.

Barnabas did this for Saul, the tent-maker from Tarsus.
Known for persecuting the early Christians, Saul had a change of
heart on the road to Damascus. There he was overcome with a vision of the risen Christ and was transformed. Few of the early
Christians had heard of this, so when they learned that Saul
planned to visit them, they were frightened. It was Barnabas who
introduced him to the others, and explained that Saul was now a
different person.

How do you find the patroning you need? You've already
taken the first step. You have learned about its importance and the
various forms it takes. *You are aware.*

The next step is *to be open to all the patroning that already happens in your life.* Your colleague says, "You gave a lively motivating
presentation," and names two strengths: your gift of motivation
and of lively presentation. Your son says, "Dad, let's play catch. It's
so much fun to play with you." There are two more gifts: a fun-
loving spirit and love of sport.

Alice Walker writes about a patroning that can occur within us.

> There are always people in history (or herstory) who
> help us, and whose "job" it is, in fact, to do this. . . .
> Sojourner Truth is one such figure for me. . . . And when
> I walk into a room of strangers who are hostile to the
> words of women, I do so with her/our cloak of author-
> ity—as black women and beloved expressions of the
> universe (i.e. children of God)—warm about me.

She smiles within my smile. That irrepressible great heart rises in my chest. Every experience that roused her passion against injustice in her lifetime shines from my eyes.

This feeling of being loved and supported by the universe in general and by certain recognizable spirits in particular is bliss. No other state is remotely like it. And perhaps that is what Jesus tried so hard to teach: that the transformation required of us is not simply to be "like" Christ, but to *be* Christ.[3]

We might ask ourselves, what "spirit helpers" are already in our souls wanting to be consulted and honored more often? And are there others whom we might invite into our beings?

Another step is to *focus on a specific need you have*. If you would like a critique of your latest poem, a reaction to your plan to upgrade the neighborhood, or a response to the store window you just decorated, ask for feedback from someone you respect.

Consider asking a person or a small group to be your patron. "What gifts do you see in me?" someone recently asked her secretary. She was surprised at the answer and the new level of understanding that grew between them.

There are more complicated questions you can ask of another. Last spring, a member of our Partners Community said that she felt muddled and confused about where she was vocationally. She hardly was able to pose a clear question, but just asked the community to listen. Its caring attentiveness and evocative questions drew her out further so that she was ready to take some next steps when they became apparent.

When you view the world as one family, you are less hesitant to ask for patroning, knowing that you may be a patron for someone else.

Patroning is not a job description but an attitude and a life-style. Once we see its importance, we can practice acting as patrons throughout our lives. There are many simple and effective ways to do this.

In Conversation: "You are a wonderful salesperson. Thanks!" A brief description of the gift you see is a good way to begin. Be ready for the person's response. You can then elaborate on your perception or add a further word of encouragement.

In Writing: A short note describing someone's gift can be stored and read again. Eight grandchildren each wrote nine reasons why they loved Grandma. Then they bound them together in a booklet. What better gift for her seventy-second birthday?

With a Gift: Knowing of Jackie's interest in cartooning, Rhoda took her to an exhibition of original cartoons. While there, Rhoda mentioned how much she enjoyed Jackie's sketches. This encouraged Jackie to use more of her drawings at work.

Patroning is not only an individual act of encouragement but also an atmosphere you create at home, in your organization, or in the community where innovation, creativity, risking new behaviors, and offering untried gifts is welcome and fostered. "What gifts would you like to use in your job . . . at home . . . at church?" is a question each of us can ask ourselves and others as we seek to enrich what we do. When we really talk about that with each other, a different level of originality and creativity is tapped.

Patroning is one of the most wonderful gifts you can give another. It is not something more to do that will burden a crowded life. It can be slipped into what you're already doing. It doesn't cost a cent, yet it is priceless. It doesn't have to take much time. "You can do it! Go for it!" takes five seconds to say but can affect a person for a lifetime.

GROUP DESIGN

Purpose: To practice patroning and being patroned.

Materials: Small labels (nine per person). We use circular labels about an inch in diameter.

A. Gathering Time, Large Group *(fifteen minutes)*

Think of someone who has been a light and encouragement to you (a teacher, parent, friend, colleague) and a specific way that person gave encouragement. Then, in turn, name the person and describe briefly (about a minute) how that person acted as your patron and encourager. (If you have more than eight people in your group, consider dividing into two groups so as not to exceed the allotted time.)

B. Sharing Groups, Groups of Four *(twenty minutes)*

Give each person a turn to share learnings from the Bible that came alive this week. Then, if there is time, speak about how it went for each of you as you compiled your list of good experiences. Don't share specific experiences at this point. We will get to that later.

C. The Label Game: Patroning One Another, Groups of Four *(sixty minutes)*

1.   Divide in new groups of four, preferably with people you do not know well. Distribute thirty-six labels to each group. In this group, each of you will speak about the three good experiences you

chose from the list you compiled individually this past week. (Session 1, Individual Work, item 2b).

2. The first person shares one of his or her good experiences. Listeners help the sharer elaborate on why this means so much and then jot on scrap paper the gifts you see in the sharer. This process is repeated for each of the good experiences.

When the person finishes sharing, each listener reads the gifts you have identified and asks the sharer to confirm or modify what was written. For example:

> "When you say you loved building a tree house with the other kids, it makes me think you have the gift of carpentry."
>
> "Well, yes, but what I really like is making things out of nothing."

The listener then writes on a label "making things out of nothing." Be on the lookout for sparks of affirmation or discovery from the sharer.

When each listener has read the gifts you have jotted down, heard feedback from the sharer, and written labels, fasten the labels on the sharer (each listener will use three labels per person).

Go around the group, using the same process for each of the four, using twenty minutes per person (fifteen minutes for sharing; five minutes for identifying, confirming, and fastening labels).

D. Learning About One Another's Gifts, Large Group (*twenty minutes*)

Regather in the large group. Each person introduces to the whole group someone in the small group by sharing some of the gifts that were discovered. Go around the circle so that all are introduced.

E. Pairing for More Patroning

1.   Read item 3 under Individual Work. Notice that you'll be doing some additional patroning with one other group member. Now is the time to make those arrangements.

2.   Then pair off on the basis of ease of meeting each other. Those who live close together or have similar schedules pair up.

3.   Then after the closing, make arrangements for meeting together for two hours before the next session if possible.

F. Closing, Large Group (*five minutes*)

Choose a way of closing that is appropriate for your group: evaluation of the session, discussion of details for the next session, song, prayer. Prayer suggestion: Those who would like to may express gratitude to God for the ways they have been patroned in this course and throughout their lives.

INDIVIDUAL WORK

Purpose: To reflect on Bible passages related to patroning and to experience patroning and being patroned.

1.   Meditate on what these passages say about patroning.

a. Paul's description of the patron (Gal. 4:19).

b. Experiences of patrons in the Bible: Barnabas (Acts 9:26–28), John the Baptist (Luke 3:1–20), Jesus (John 14:12–29 and Luke 22:31–34).

2.   Journal on these questions: What kind of patroning do I need at this time? From whom? What kind of patroning can I give? To whom?

3.   In-depth patroning (*Note:* This assignment requires extra time because it involves getting together with another person. Those who take the time to do this find it extremely valuable):

a. Meet with the person you selected (in Group Design E) for at least two hours.

b. Depending on your time, describe to each other all twenty good experiences or simply those you like best. The following is an example of how to proceed. George describes one good experience, Mary listens and helps George elaborate. As this happens, Mary writes down items under this heading, "George is happy when . . . he is innovating . . . he is up front and on stage . . . he is walking in the woods alone," etc.

Do this for about forty minutes. Mary reads the list of gifts she has made and asks George to confirm, clarify, or modify. For example, George might say, "Yes, I'm happy walking in the woods alone. Actually, I love being alone in all sorts of situations—outdoors, inside with a good book, etc." After Mary's list, "George is happy when . . . ," is refined by both, then Mary, with George's help, tries to name and identify some of the gifts indicated by the list. For example, "You have a gift for solitude," or "You seem to love to be a pioneer," or "You are an occasion maker," or "You have a gift for relaxing and helping others relax." When you have completed that process, reverse it and let George become the patron-listener as Mary describes her list of good experiences. Be sure to budget half your time for each person. It is disappointing if a disproportionate amount of time is used on one person.

    c. After you part, reflect more on your overall impression of your partner's gifts. Summarize your impressions in a note to be mailed to your partner or given at the next session. Notice any consistent abilities that flow through your partner's life—e.g., "Bill, your love of adventure comes through in a lot of situations." These notes are an important part of the process and are usually cherished by the recipients.

    4. At the end of the week, summarize in writing your work with this assignment.

SESSION 3

Which Vision Is Mine to Carry?

When Martin Luther King, Jr., cried out, "I have a dream," and then spelled out his vision for America, the nation was electrified. We were hungry for vision. His was clear:

> I have a dream that my four little children will one day live in a nation where they will not be judged by the color of their skin but by the content of their character.[1]

King wanted to view the world from God's perspective. Then he tried to live it for our times. This is what we all are given to do: to be immersed in God's dream for the world and to carry out part of it in our time and place. This session describes the importance of vision and the difference between vision and call. Then it helps you discover which part of God's vision is deeply implanted in your heart.

In *Living Toward a Vision*, theologian Walter Brueggemann summarizes God's dream as described in the Bible:

> The central vision of world history in the Bible is that all creation is one, every creature in community with every other, living in harmony and security toward the joy and well-being of every other creature. . . . The most staggering expression of the vision is that *all persons are children of a single family*, members of a single tribe, heirs of a single hope, and bearers of a single destiny, namely, the care and management of all of God's creation.[2]

The disciples, after Jesus' death, were convinced that they were carriers of this vision. They were fired by these words from the prophet Joel:

. . . I will pour out my Spirit upon all flesh,
and your sons and your daughters shall prophesy,
and the young shall see visions,
and the old shall dream dreams;
yea, and on my manservants and my maidservants in those days
I will pour out my Spirit; and they shall prophesy.
(Acts 2:17, 18)[3]

Using this passage, Peter showed that God wants to pour the Spirit on everyone: young, old, male, female, rich, poor. All are included. When that happens, people see visions, dream dreams, and are able to embody and articulate God's vision of the oneness of all creation.

The disciples experienced an outpouring of the Spirit that catapulted them into a life of committed action to spread the love they had experienced so deeply with Jesus.

The New Testament describes individuals who implemented particular aspects of this love. Luke, the doctor, focused on healing and wholeness and wrote from that perspective. Fisherman Peter, who had left his nets to follow Jesus, emphasized the importance of individuals knowing God. Tent-maker Paul, in his later years, devoted his life to encouraging the growth of communities of believers.

We can appreciate the fullness of God's *vision*, but are given a piece of that vision to carry and live as our own.

If indeed we are entrusted with part of God's vision, it is important to try to discover what it is. By definition, it will express biblical themes that contain the vision: love, justice, wholeness, reconciliation. But because we are human beings, our particular piece of the vision will be specific and derived from our unique experience, makeup, and abilities. It will take shape out of the combination of who we are and what we have experienced.

In addition to seeing how our piece of the vision relates to God's vision, it is clarifying to differentiate vision from call (which is discussed more fully in the next session). As we use the terms, vision is seeing or believing something; call is doing something. Unlike vision, which is usually large and seemingly impossible, call is specific, imaginable, feasible. Vision can be consistent over long periods, even a lifetime; call changes with circumstances. Vision is seeing the big picture; call is the way we implement the vision in a particular time and place.

King saw the big picture:

> There is no separate black path to power and fulfillment that does not have to intersect with white roots. Somewhere along the way the two must join together, black and white together, we shall overcome, and I still believe it.[4]

He thought this was the way we all should live our lives.

> You ought to believe something in life, believe that thing so fervently that you will stand up with it to the end of your days.[5]

The way King lived his vision varied with the circumstances: pastoring Dexter Avenue Baptist Church in Atlanta; organizing integration efforts in the South; then confronting the nation; finally working for peace among nations.

For her whole life, Jean Adams has had a passion for including people who feel like outsiders. This has been expressed in many calls. Living in an interracial neighborhood in Philadelphia, she built up the spirit of harmony through working on community dances and parties. As an art teacher in the public schools, she always gave special attention to the ones who did not fit in. Now retired, she offers her art-making skills to help adults find lost parts of themselves.

Lester Brown, director of Worldwatch Institute, envisions a planet free from environmental degradation.[6] His call was to found and now direct the Institute that researches the issues and produces annual "State of the World" reports.[7] Jackie's nephew, Greg, in his twenties, has the same vision. His call at the present time is to work for the Forest Service in Arizona.

You can see our working definitions of "vision" and "call." There is much fluidity and variety in how they are manifested in people's lives. And, of course, not everyone's life lends itself to being described by these terms.

Circumstance can shape our vision and thrust us into a call. In high school, actor/dancer David Kamens captured leading parts in plays and musicals. Enrolled in a school for the arts, and believing in the power of drama and the arts to give meaning to life, he was headed for a theater vocation. Then illness struck. When told he had AIDS, he left school to learn all he could about this disease. Then he traveled the country speaking and teaching as an AIDS educator. He wished for a world without AIDS, of course. But in the time that he had, he held the vision that all people could understand this illness and relate with sensitivity to those afflicted.

To discover the vision we are given to carry requires that we *open ourselves to receive it or to allow it to unfold*. Put yourself in God's presence. Ask what area of need is yours to address. Look for signposts that point you to vision.

One signpost is our own passion. Insight comes when we *reflect on what evokes our most passionate criticism, our deepest grief, or what energizes us to new possibilities*. Certain situations or events make us more angry than others; certain pictures or articles in the paper touch deep chords; certain visions draw our allegiance. When we pay attention to them, we get glimmers of a dream that will not let us go or a central concern that has gripped us for a long time.

Some people come to know their vision gradually and without much difficulty. But for others, discovering an aspect of God's vision that is theirs to carry is not an easy task. Because problems are so complex, we tend to block them out or think the experts will solve them. The result is a psychic numbing that leads to pervasive ignorance and apathy: "I don't know and I don't care." Yet regardless of size, no current problem is without solutions. What is lacking is personal and political will to solve them.

In *Despair and Personal Power in a Nuclear Age*, Joanna Macy tells of finding many who are truly fearful that the planet itself might not survive. Because of the enormity of that fear, they mask it in consumerism, individualism, and a passivity that is no longer shockable.[8] In her workshops, Macy helps people name and feel their fears, and then to share them. In that sharing with others, there is a deep bonding that occurs, a solidarity that we are in this together. This produces energy to imagine what the planet would look like if it truly flourished. Ignited by that vision, participants are then invited to plan steps to move toward that vision.

Her process gives us clues to how we can be in touch with a life-giving vision. Whether or not we are readily in touch with our vision, her wisdom adds depth to our reflections. *Face our pain for the world and ourselves*, Macy would counsel. In emotions like anger, outrage, or despair there is tremendous creativity. But first the darkness must be confronted. Macy quotes philosopher Jacob Needleman on facing the unknown. It is there

> in that fleeting state between dreams, which is called "despair" in some Western teachings and "self-questioning" in Eastern traditions, [that] a person is said to be able to receive the truth, both about nature and his [or her] own possible role in the universal order.[9]

Not only must we face our fear, we must *name our despair*, if that is within us.

This deep questioning may make us feel alone. It is what leads some people to a *wilderness experience*. Before Jesus was able to state his vision publicly, he spent forty days in the desert wrestling with options, praying, listening to and sorting the voices—which were of God and which were not. When we go apart, and place ourselves before the Spirit, we are ready for new perspectives.

When faced with unexpected challenges, our vision can prove to be too small or weak. Then it becomes necessary to *learn from those whose vision is more fully adjusted to present circumstance*. To read about them or see them at work refocuses our vision. We may be disturbed or frightened, for example, about environmental degradation and be bereft of vision. Yet if, for example, we expose ourselves to the work of Lester Brown and his Worldwatch Institute, we will cultivate our ability to dream of a world that works.

Speaking of our pain or despair as well as our hopes, dreams, and visions with other concerned people unleashes our passion. Sharing also releases our power to remember and resubscribe to God's dream of a thriving people in a flourishing world of justice and compassion.

Actually *picturing what your vision would look like* if it happened also energizes you to start making it happen. That is what Quaker Elise Boulding has done regarding peace. She asks people to imagine a world without weapons.

A vision is not easily sustained; it must be nurtured. This happens when we not only learn from people of vision, but also when we share our vision with one another. At a seminary workshop, faculty and students were asked to remember the vision that first brought them to the seminary. Then they reflected on how their vision was fostered by the courses they were studying or teaching. Said one, "I came to this lunch frantic with pressure, but I'm leaving deeply touched by what I found within myself and heard from others about why we're here together at seminary." Participants were refreshed and renewed.

Failure to nurture our vision can cause burnout. In 1979, a *Time* magazine story about Pehr Gyllenhammar, then president of Volvo in Sweden, caught our eye. Beginning in his own company and then going around the world, he was addressing what he termed a growing problem for industrial nations, "the mismatch between people and jobs." People need to know why they are doing a particular job and the value it has in the larger scheme of things. Said Gyllenhammar, "The problem today is not just to pay people, but also to help them feel they can identify with something in society."[10]

It is not uncommon for people in our groups to say they do not have vision. Vision is a gift; not everyone has it. However, it is possible for everyone to appreciate vision and join in implementing it when appropriate.

One reason that people do not have a sense of vision is that the dreams they have had in the past have been dashed. Vision can be fragile. If we put forward a vision and are made to feel foolish, or if we work for a dream and our efforts end in failure, our ability to envision is wounded. Our vision can be renewed if we open ourselves to healing. To do that, we have found these questions from Jean Houston fruitful:

✤ What happened? How were you wounded?

✤ What did you feel when you were wounded?

✤ What were the full consequences of this wounding in your life, for good and ill?

✤ In the light of this, what do you want?

✤ What does this mean? What pattern is playing itself out here?[11]

As you ponder these questions, preferably in writing, an area of disappointment or pain can become the source of insight and the renewal of your sense of vision.

Being aware and responsible for part of God's vision need not involve long-term commitments to a certain institution or work. Making God's care and love available to people under stress is one way to state Jessie Daniels's vision. A woman in her seventies, she is ready to share a book, offer a meal, or give someone a ride to the hospital. Jessie is delighted to be a companion and helper to all kinds of people who cross her path.

What we are talking about need not involve doing something different, but rather seeing differently what we do. As an old story goes: Two stonemasons are asked what they are doing. One replies, "Laying stone." But the other says, "I'm building a cathedral."

Job, relationships, parenting—all aspects of life take on a different hue when seen as part of God's vision. Allowing all of life to reflect this vision is a process that takes time. It is unwise to rush the process or to oversimplify it. People in our groups sometimes are disappointed when they do not know their vision by the end of the six-week course. We, on the other hand, are happy if people *begin* to explore this tremendous concept within that brief time.

Some of us may never feel that a particular vision has our name on it. What we all can do is grow in our ability to bring God's vision to every endeavor in which we are engaged.

GROUP DESIGN

Purpose: To become conscious of and share our sense of vision.

Materials: Candle, wooden matches, low table.

A. Gathering Time, Large Group (*ten minutes*)

Put on a perky jazz or ragtime record. One person acts as Simple Simon and does motions to the rhythm of the record, one consistent motion for about thirty seconds, then another motion. The group imitates. The purpose of this is simply to loosen up and have some fun together. With a stretch of the imagination, it can be seen as related to vision in that it depends on Simple Simon having a vision of the group as fun-loving.

B. Sharing Groups, Groups of Four (*twenty minutes*)

Share your experiences with patroning. Exchange patroning notes and, if you like, read them to one another.

C. "I Have a Dream," Individuals and Groups of Four (*sixty minutes*)

1. Journaling. Individuals (fifteen minutes). Encourage each person to become settled and quiet in a comfortable position with notebook and pen ready. Give a short review of the session material on vision. Then invite people to jot down any glimmers they have about their own sense of vision. To stimulate this, read the following material slowly and meditatively, pausing at length where indicated. Give people plenty of time to think and write:

"How can we figure out which piece of God's vision is ours? This is what we want to begin to do right now. While I'm talking, jot down in your notebook what occurs to you.

"What is it that concerns you very much, has concerned you for a long time, perhaps even from childhood or teen years? (*Pause.*)

"What excites you to great joy, hope, possibilities . . . but also causes high frustration, even pain, or envy? (*Pause.*)

"What is it that makes you angry, moves you to tears, keeps you awake at night? (*Pause.*)

"Look at your choice of reading—books, magazines, newspaper articles. What subjects move you the most? Which do you turn to most frequently? (*Pause.*)

"If you were to look at the area that concerns you most and have a dream about how that could be better or different or new, what would your dream be? (*Pause.*)"

2. Sharing. Groups of Four (forty-five minutes). Now we will have a chance to share our vision in a special way. Move into groups of four (we suggest people you have not been with before). Find a place in the building where you can lie down on the floor, each on his or her back, with heads touching in the middle like spokes of a wheel. This sounds slightly wacky, but if everyone is game, give it a try. (An alternative is to sit in chairs, back-to-back in fours, but the first suggestion is preferable.) Depending on the space, if you are crowded, you might like to have groups in different rooms. Here are the instructions for sharing:

a. Settle yourselves, relax, enjoy this position, ask God for guidance, and be silent for a few minutes.

b. As you feel moved, one person share your vision briefly. You may have something quite definite. You may have only a glimmer or a hint. Share what you can.

c. The others listen to that sharing, and then each in turn walks into the speaker's dream as if it were a reality. Participate in it. Don't discuss it, give advice, or say it's impossible. Imagine that you share the speaker's enthusiasm and concern. Add to their dream from your perspective. If you as a listener need clarification about the nature of the vision, ask for that. Then simply in a few words affirm the dream in any way that's genuine. This is challenging. It isn't easy to get out of yourself and into another's dream. Here is an example of how this might work out:

First Person: I see a church which has set up a Council of Elders, people over 70 or 75, who come together regularly to offer their wisdom on current problems. There is a sense of honoring their experience and including them fully in the life of the church.

Second Person: As I walk into your dream I think of the inadequate health care system in this country. But moving past that, I imagine a way for adult children to keep their parents at home by having long-term financial aid for professional help, rather then having it available only for nursing home residents.

Third Person: I'm finding it hard to dream because my father just died, and I'm grieving. But I affirm your longing and maybe soon I'll be actively working on the problems of the aging. I've had a wealth of experience in the last two years in caring for Dad.

Fourth Person: I feel I have my hands full being a board member. I know I can't take on anything else, but if you do want to do something, I'll do all I can to obtain the backing of the board.

d. When you have had the first round, go to the second
person, and so on, until each is finished. Allow about
ten minutes for each round. Try to budget the time
for each person. If you concentrate on the first one,
there will not be time left for the others. When you're
finished, spend some time in silence.

Briefly record any new insights concerning your vision as a result of this sharing.

3.   Group Sharing. Large Group (fifteen minutes). Whole
group reconvene around a lighted candle, either on the floor or on
a low table. Beside it are some wooden matches. One by one, each
person take a match, light it from the candle, and, while the
match burns, briefly describe the vision that you shared in the
group of four.

D. Closing, Large Group (*ten minutes*)

Choose one or two of the following suggestions as appropriate
for your group: evaluation of session, discussion of details for next
session, prayer and/or song ("This Little Light of Mine").

INDIVIDUAL WORK

Purpose: To ponder biblical passages related to vision; to do further personal work on vision, patroning, and gifts.

1.   Meditate on what these passages say about vision:

✤ its importance (Prov. 29:18);

✤ who receives it and how (Acts 2:14–24);

✤ having a piece of a vision (Acts 10);

✤ its substance (Isa. 58);

✤ its breadth (Ps. 117);

✤ its timing (Hab. 2:2–3).

2. Further work:

a. *On vision:* Reflect further on the vision you shared in the group. Continue the writing you started in the session. Add further insights. Try to record how the others "walked" into your dream. What of significance did they add to it? Did anyone's response deflect you from your vision? What can be learned from that?

b. *On patroning:* Give the note you wrote on your partner's gifts to that person if you have not already done so.

c. *On your own gifts:* Ponder the note you received and any other insights as you review your work on gifts: the sketch you did in the first group design, your own list of good experiences and what came out of that for you, your patron's responses, the labels from the group session. Summarize your findings using these phrases as a guide:

My strongest gifts are . . .

The ones I enjoy most are . . .

3. Gift identification brings delight and difficulty. For a greater understanding of what blocks the evoking of gifts, read the following section "Why We Bury Our Talents."

4. For further clarification of how a Christian community can help or hinder the process we are describing, read "The Gift-Evoking Process in the Community."

5. Summarize in writing what you did with this assignment.

The Gift-Evoking Process in the Community.   The Bible assures us that if we wish to accept gifts, the Spirit gives them to each of us. They are within us. Here are things that we and the community can do to call them forth.

Identify Gifts: The more specific we can be in this, the better. Jim has the gift of writing. But what kind of writing? He gets the most fun out of writing on demand for groups who have an immediate use for what he offers.

Confirm Gifts: When Jim's community asks him to write something for it, his gift is confirmed. His creativity flowers. Lack of confirmation may signal that the community is not ready for my gift or that my gift is not yet ready for the community. It needs development and polishing.

Accept Your Own Gifts: There are powerful personal and social forces working against accepting our gifts. We have been taught not to be proud, not to brag. Some of us have been in subordinate positions and have been conditioned to hold back.

Offer Gifts: Don't hide them. Offer them, even if they are not fully developed. Once you start using them, the gifts will mature.

Promote Each Other's Gifts: A store owner exhibited sculptures done by a friend. She announced the opening, planned a reception, and in this way fostered the sculptor's gift and created a way for others to do so as well. Receiving another's gift requires openness and thought, even ingenuity. It is an essential part of gift-evoking.

Why We Bury Our Talents.   If you're having difficulty identifying your gifts, consider this checklist.

1. Have you asked God for help in recognizing and using your gifts?

2. Do you have a person or small group that encourages you to identify and use gifts?

3. Are you afraid of rejection if you use your gifts?

4. Are you allowing only those gifts you think will be accepted to be named and refusing to identify the core gifts?

5. Are you afraid of provoking envy if you use your gifts?

6. Does your envy toward others cause you to focus on their accomplishments and block you from developing your gifts?

7. Gifts imply specific commitment to use them. Are you avoiding commitment? Why?

8. Do you back off from the pain and work of creativity?

9. Are you afraid if you try something new it will threaten other people and cause tension? Are you willing to move through that tension?

10. Are you unwilling to use a gift until you are mature in it, an expert? If so, is it because you are taking your gifts too seriously? Are you afraid of experimenting, failing, playing, looking silly?

SESSION 4

What Is God Calling Me to Do?

All children can thrive. That's Beth Burns's vision, pure and simple. And her call is to create a ballet company for inner-city youngsters in Santa Ana, California, to build their confidence and call forth their creative abilities.

A central theme in the Christian tradition is that God calls people to special work, specific action that implements their vision. *Call* or *calling* is something more than working to pay the bills or taking a volunteer job because it needs doing, important as these are. It implies deeper motivation, hearing a voice and responding. To people of faith, it is God who calls. People who sense a call also listen to the voice of their own experience and the needs of the times.

This session offers both current and biblical examples of call and then describes how we can position ourselves to hear and respond to call.

When Beth Burns taught high school in a suburban neighborhood, she was unhappy. Her lifework did not have a focus. Summer was approaching, and she began dreaming about how she could serve the poor. Her ideas were limited to what she thought would work and at which she could not fail. Then, one night in bed, putting aside those cautions she asked, "If I could do anything (and not worry about money or skill), what would it be?" A clear answer came. "Transform people's lives through the beauty of dance." Beth elaborates, "I have always seen dance as a deep, beautiful, spiritual thing, like the freedom of heaven.

"Once I heard the answer inside myself, it rang. It had a quality of energy I could not turn my back on. I had learned what question to ask to hear a call."

From her youngest days, dance has been important to Beth. Through the discipline of practice and the exhilaration of performance, she learned to express herself. These were gifts she knew she could offer. Through reading, learning, and listening to friends who were working in the neighborhood of St. Joseph School in Santa Ana, she and a friend, Nageeba Colarossi, decided to offer free dance classes and a chance to perform during the summer. After the neighborhood performance, she reports, "It was clear from the children's faces that this was important for them, so I decided to make it a year-round thing." From a book on grant writing, she learned how to articulate the need she saw and the answer she proposed. Her mission statement included these words:

> To develop self-esteem, self-discipline, and a sense of achievement with children who cannot afford opportunities to develop their talent.

The St. Joseph Ballet Company started with twenty children that first summer. Eight years later it had grown to include fifteen hundred children directly through its year-round classes and eighteen thousand others through its outreach programs in public schools.

Beth provides more than dance. Her studio is a safe place where the children know they are loved. In this atmosphere, their confidence rises, their gifts are fostered, and they have the heady experience of developing an art they have come to love. Each year the company mounts major productions with such enticing titles as "Child of Grace," "See the Love," and "The Sky and My Soul." In 1991 they performed a ballet written by a young author, with sets designed by a young artist, to music by a young composer.

Beth celebrates the potential within the inner city by lifting up the "flowers that can and do grow if we only water them a bit." This experience has been "a thrilling adventure of faith. Not only is this call a gift to me, I receive on a daily basis rewards of glow-ing faces of children who are thrilled."

So many people's work dehumanizes them, notes Beth. "I have a pure sense of peace. I am living my life just as I had hoped. The biggest context of this work is faith and my relationship with God. It is the means through which God communicates with me. Once you know where you're going, you get this deep gut-level energy. Then it is simply a question of how to solve the problems that come up. Here I have been blessed. I have found over and over again that exactly what I needed was there. This is a 'we' thing—there is a real sense of community in what we are doing. People are there to help."[1]

Similar experiences of call are described by biblical writers. God calls people to relationship with God and to specific roles and tasks, both to be and to do. Alone on a mountain Moses ex-perienced the presence of God and then heard his name called—"Moses! Moses!"—and answered, "Here I am." "I will send you to Pharaoh to lead my people, the Israelites, out of Egypt" (Exod. 3:4, 10, NAB).

Does God call everyone? Isn't a sense of that calling reserved for the few?

In the Bible there is a gradual expansion of the understanding of call. At first reserved for the Hebrew people and then to faith-ful people within the tribe, the idea of call develops to include all nations and peoples. Isaiah expresses this:

> All you who are thirsty,
> come to the water.
> *(Isa. 55:1, NAB)*

While presenting God's call as being offered to all, the Bible includes colorful and informative details about why we may not feel as if we are included in that call. God is not portrayed as going after the best qualified for a particular job. Youthful, inexperienced David was summoned to fight the terrible giant Goliath. Mary, an obscure young woman, was chosen to be the mother of Jesus. Wobbly, impetuous Peter was called to a ministry of fearless preaching, witnessing, and healing.

Sometimes the person called is overcome with a sense of unworthiness. Peter's first response to Christ's call was "Leave me, Lord. I am a sinful man" (Luke. 5:8, NAB). Isaiah felt much the same way: "I am lost, for I am a man of unclean lips" (Isa. 6:5, JB). At the news of his own calling, Jeremiah protested, "Ah, Lord Yahweh; look, I do not know how to speak: I am a child!" (Jer. 1:6, JB).

Responding to call sometimes has a sense of exhilaration about it such as Beth Burns experienced. But it also can involve struggle, especially when implementing it brings resistance and opposition. Never has this been more poignantly expressed than by Jeremiah.

> For the word of God has become for me
> a reproach and derision all day long.
> If I say, "I will not mention God,
> or speak any more in God's name,"
> there is in my heart, as it were, a burning fire
> shut up in my bones,
> and I am weary with holding it in,
> and I cannot.
> (Jer. 20:8–9)[2]

According to psychiatrist Carl G. Jung, to heed one's inner voice or the voice of God within is a vocation.[3] Jung described from a psychological perspective why this involves struggle. It requires that we free ourselves from societal expectations and listen quietly for inner guidance. No special talent or genius is required. What is needed is openness to listen and courage to follow the guidance that comes. The choice is ours: to respond to the inner summons or to follow the crowd; to cultivate and trust our inward authority or to rely solely on external authority. For much of our early life, we are schooled, churched, and governed to adjust to what the culture requires. It is not easy to hear or walk to a different drumbeat.

How can we position ourselves to hear and respond to a call?

First, as has been mentioned, we must go *within*. There we become conscious of the presence of God and wait. We can ask for a call and open ourselves to guidance. Perhaps one step will occur to us. If we take that, another may open up.

Paul's experience illustrates this (see Acts 9). On the road to Damascus he was first given a vision of the reality of the risen Christ; then he was directed to go to the city; there he was told what to do. Ananias, who was also following the guidance he had received in a dream, indicated the next step for Paul.

We don't assume that our first enthusiastic idea is necessarily a genuine call. We stay open. We may nourish our openness to the inner summons by reading about others who are living out of a sense of call.

Listening to our own deep yearnings, hopes, struggles, and objections, we bring them to God. We attempt to examine our willingness to be open versus our wish for instant clarity.[4]

"I'd love to have a sense of being called by God to do something" is a remark heard frequently in our groups. We can begin by asking: Am I listening? Do I make room in my life for that? Is my mind and schedule so busy that I cannot quiet the automatic parade of thoughts and listen for something different?

Open Yourself to Circumstance: Let it shape your call. One of our participants who was terminally ill when she took this course knew she had only a short time to live. She felt moved to work with doctors to raise their awareness of how patients deal personally with approaching death.

In 1955, James Rouse co-authored a plan for the redevelopment of Washington, D.C., called *No Slums in Ten Years*: It was ignored. Clearly ahead of his time, Rouse turned his attention for a time to the suburbs. But when cities were ready to talk with him, he was instrumental in renewing downtown areas such as Baltimore's Inner Harbor.[5]

Consult People Currently Active in Your Area of Call: This can be done through reading or personal contact. You will understand the realities of what is being done, what needs doing, and how you could fit in. That can help you sharpen your call. If you volunteer in the area that interests you, that firsthand experience will also help.

Test Your Sense of Call with Someone Else or a Group: Their questions and responses will make you think and probe more deeply. If you tell a friend or colleague that you feel moved to do a particular project and you receive a weak response, pay attention. You may not be clear enough within or ready for action.

The timing of call differs from person to person. When Maruja Candano took this course in Mexico City, she was ready for a call. A lawyer, she had given up that work while raising her children. As they grew older and she could consider returning to work, her husband, Gerardo, became ill with cancer. Learning of the attitudinal healing techniques pioneered by psychiatrist Gerald Jampolsky[6] in California, she and Gerardo put them to work in their lives. Eventually Gerardo was declared free of cancer, and Maruja wanted to share their learnings with others. While working with the material in this session, a call came loud and clear: start an attitudinal healing center in Mexico City.

This she did. She, Gerardo, and other volunteers were trained by members of the California center. Now they help ill people approach life with a positive attitude so that they can live productively despite their illness, and in some cases receive physical healing.

Some calls take a long time to clarify and develop. Several years ago, Jim Hunter, a successful small businessman, was jokingly asked what he wanted to be when he grew up. Turning pensive, he replied, "You know, I've always wanted to run for office. My sister is a school-board member in Pennsylvania, and I have such a strong interest in local affairs that I think I'd like to hold office in some capacity." About ten years later, the time was right. Jim ran and won a position on the Arlington County Board. In that ten-year period, service with the Arlington Housing Corporation, activities with refugees, participation in United Way and the YMCA all gave Jim added experience to bring to the County Board.

Now a call within that call is developing for Jim.

> About two weeks ago, I woke up at 5:30 AM thinking about how to include minority groups more fully into the life stream of our community. It occurred to me that I'm in a unique position to incorporate them in the political process, to give them more responsibility, and to help their leaders ready themselves to hold office. Few black, Hispanic . . . Vietnamese citizens now know how to do this.

Jim is particularly eager to work with people ages twenty to thirty-five to introduce them to the "old-time political operatives," to get them appointed to commissions, and to widen their exposure, so that when they are ready to run for office, they will know how. "I feel called to do this," says Jim. "I have a deep fervent belief that this will empower minority groups and weave the rich multicultural fabric of Arlington more tightly, so we'll have a more beautiful community because of their active involvement."

Feelings about call vary a great deal. Theologian and author Frederick Buechner writes: "The place God calls you to is the place where your deep gladness and the world's deep hunger meet."[7] Sometimes a call does fill us with delight. On the other hand, it might surprise or frighten us until we get used to it. We may say, "If I really am open to that voice within, I'm afraid I'll be asked to do something I really don't want to do." Are we imagining a god who is against us?

Certainly a call may stretch and challenge us, but an authentic call is something we really want to do, something that expresses what is deep within us.

Jesus thought of God as a loving parent who desires the very best for us (Luke 11:1–13). If it is God who calls, we can be confident that the call will help us develop more fully in ways that give joy and help to others as well as to ourselves.

"Stick your neck out" is the motto for the Giraffe Project, headquartered in Langley (pop. 700) on picturesque Whidbey Island, north of Seattle.[8] The project identifies people who stick their necks out for the common good and who do this with an adventurous nature and good humor despite the risk; then it names them as Giraffes and sends along a scroll of congratulations. In its newsletter, "The Giraffe Gazette," and on television spots, the project goes all out to publicize its stories. All this is to inspire everyone "to stop being an ostrich," according to founders John Graham and Anne Medlock.[9]

Though Graham and Medlock do not use the term "call," they celebrate people of courage who feel moved to change things for the better. Like seventy-one-year-old former teacher Carrie Barefoot Dickerson, who waged a nine-year battle to block the construction of a nuclear power plant in Oklahoma. Or student Tanya Vogt, who led fellow students in banning Styrofoam from their high school and is now pushing national fast-food chains to give up "the everlasting stuff." Or Janet Marchase, who created the Down's Syndrome Adoption Exchange, "placing hundreds of newborn Down's syndrome infants in loving families by working double shifts as a waitress to pay the Exchange's bills."[10]

Say Giraffe founders Graham and Medlock, "There's something each of us can do to make the world a better place."[11] Putting ideals into action—that is what call is all about.

GROUP DESIGN

Purpose: To reflect on the experience of call today and in the Bible.

Materials: Marking pens, newsprint.

A. Gathering Time, Large Group (*fifteen minutes*)

Large group stand in a circle. Turn to the right and massage the shoulders of the person in front of you. After a few minutes, turn in the opposite direction and do the same.

B. Sharing Groups, Groups of Four (*thirty minutes*)

Choose from these suggestions for sharing:

✤ your learnings from the Bible;

✤ insights or questions that came from reading "Why We Bury Our Talents" and "The Gift-Evoking Process in the Community";

✛ personal discoveries you made about patroning, vision, and call.

C. Experiences of Call in the Bible and Today, Small Groups (*thirty minutes*)

1. Divide the large group into six small groups (two or more to a group).

2. Each small group select a biblical description of call. Choose from the calls of Samuel (1 Sam. 3:1–18), Moses (Exod. 3, 4:1–23), Isaiah (Isa. 6), Jeremiah (Jer. 1:4–19), the disciples (Luke 5:1–11), Paul (Acts 9:1–30), or other biblical persons of your choosing.

3. Read over the passage together silently and then discuss these questions:

✛ In what circumstances did call happen?

✛ To whom?

✛ What did it feel like?

✛ What did it involve?

✛ What kinds of reactions were evoked when the called person tried to implement the call?

4. Each small group then prepare to present to the larger group:

✛ the name of your story and a quick summary of it;

✛ learnings about call from your story that are relevant for you today.

D. Group Presentations on Call, Large Group (*thirty minutes*)

1.   Each small group share its presentation of the story summary and learnings about call.

2.   Optional: After each presentation, consider writing learnings about call on newsprint.

E. Closing, Large Group (*fifteen minutes*)

Choose one or two of the following as appropriate for your group: evaluation of session, discussion of details for next session, song and/or prayer of thanks for those who have heard God's call and for our own openness to that call.

INDIVIDUAL WORK

Purpose: To meditate on Jesus' experience with call and to ponder your own call and possible next steps.

1.   Read and meditate daily on Luke 4 to gain insight on how Jesus clarified and issued his call and how people responded to it.

2.   Clarify your thoughts and feelings about call by doing some journal writing. Begin by using one or more of the following responses. Then expand your thoughts and feelings.

✛ I don't want to think about it.

✛ It's exciting.

✛ It's scary.

✛ I don't believe God has a calling for me.

✤ I'm not good enough to receive a call.

✤ I'd like to feel called, but I don't hear any call.

✤ I hear a call but don't know what to do about it.

✤ I'm confused.

✤ Other.

3.   Consider possible next steps regarding call. *If you don't hear a call:*

✤ Is there a block to your hearing it?

✤ Are you devoting enough time to listening for it?

✤ Are you rejecting the call that is there in favor of something more to your immediate liking?

If you do have a sense of calling:

✤ Is there something further to do with it?

✤ Is this a time to ponder or clarify more?

✤ Should you take a step alone?

✤ Is now the time to go public?

✤ Is there something else you could do?

4.   In light of these reflections, decide on an appropriate next step, write it out, and tell your patron about it.

5.   Summarize in writing what you did with this assignment.

Note: Have a try at all these questions or concentrate on those that seem particularly appropriate for you. Remember there are no "right" answers. The important thing is to deal honestly and openly with the material. Don't be too concerned about your feelings. Some people feel encouraged in this course; some discover envy as others have "breakthroughs" and they don't. Remember that God works within you in the timing and manner that best suits you. When some people take these courses, nothing hits them at the time. Later, as their life and circumstances change, material from the course reappears and becomes relevant. If you respond to the questions during the course and deal with them personally, no matter how you feel, the chances are good that the insight that is most important to you will recur when you need it.

SESSION 5

How Can I Work Together
with Those Who Share My Call?

If you're moved by a call and want to follow it, not only alone but with others, your task is to find those who share your call and to organize effectively. How to do that is the subject of this session.

Up to this point we have been mainly concerned with individual discernment, choices, and actions. Now we focus on the dynamics of organizing and belonging to a small group that responds to a common call. In the next session we explore how the larger community—your church, school, or workplace—can support the callings of its members.

You may be in one of several places as you reach this point in our process. You might realize you need more time to discover your call. Or, recognizing that the very idea of call presupposes a relationship with God, you might wish to focus on nourishing that.

On the other hand, you might have clarity about your sense of calling. This might entail bringing a new project into being as did Beth Burns. Or you may realize, "What I'm already doing I now see as a calling." This might be your work, family life, or service at church or in the community. Or you may need to focus on a temporary call such as an illness, care for an elderly parent, or a transition.

In any of these situations you may want to band together with others to pursue your call. This can be a significant act. Margaret Mead's words ring with power:

> Never doubt that a small group of thoughtful, commit-
> ted people can change the world. Indeed, it's the only
> thing that ever has.[1]

Christian history abounds with examples of this truth. Fran-
ciscans confronted the world with their passionate concern for
simplicity. Tiny groups of Quakers cut through the morass of ec-
clesial structures and encouraged people to rediscover direct experience of the Spirit. Members of the Confessing Church in
Germany put their lives on the line against Hitler's monstrous
schemes. Base communities in Mexico, with no money, power, or
prestige, sat on the floor of the President's waiting room until their
demand for clean village water was granted. Throughout history
tiny groups such as these, refusing defeat, are expressions of call
carried out together to meet the needs of the times. Operating
without fanfare, they have carried hope, compassion, and faith to
successive generations.

A fundamental lesson from these experiences is that God
works not only through individuals but also through communities.
To live a call communally may seem very appealing. However,
there is no guarantee that companions who wish to walk the same
path will surface immediately.

At times we are called to be alone in the desert with no supports except God. We need these periods, whether we welcome
them or not, to relate solely to God without the company of
others.

When we are given companions, the way we work with and
relate to them can make the difference between whether our as-
sociation is creative or depleting. It is possible to organize in ways
that prevent many of the problems that sometimes plague such
groups.[2] What is needed are group forms and procedures that
honor each person's contribution, allow for both solitary and

communal ways of going about things, and accomplish tasks effectively and with good spirit.

A beautiful way of organizing was demonstrated by Jesus and the small band of disciples willing to live, learn, pray, and work with him. This little group succeeded and failed and tried again. After Jesus' death, it was remarkably strengthened in its ability to spread what he lived and taught. No one could have predicted the amazing change this tiny group of committed people would set in motion.

The term *servant community* describes the kind of small group that has deep roots in our tradition. The word *community* reminds us of our solidarity with one another and God. *Servant* implies that we are brought together by the call to serve one another and others. A servant community incorporates a creative combination of prayer, caring, and task. It is like a church in microcosm.

A variety of forms for servant communities work well depending on your purpose.

A *mission group* is composed of people who want to work together on the same project.

A *support group* consists of those who wish to help one another discern, grow, or be faithful in the different life challenges each faces.

A *committee turned into a community* is appropriate when committee members wish to add spiritual development and community building activities to their common effort.

What follows are learnings about procedure from our experience with servant communities. They are offered not as a blueprint but for your own thinking. Trust God's guidance and your own creativity as you move through the steps. Our suggestions have to do with getting started, inviting participation, organizing and sustaining, and incorporating change. These suggestions are for starting a new group but also can be adapted to existing groups.

✤ Getting Started ✤

Oddly enough, if you want to carry out your call communally, you may need to begin on your own, taking whatever action you prayerfully discern you can do. Trust the wisdom in Goethe's words:

> Whatever you can do, or dream you can, begin it.
> Boldness has genius, power and magic in it.[3]

When you are doing something you really want to do, your enthusiasm is contagious. Many communities are born when people are drawn to a person who is doing what he or she passionately believes in. That person's fire attracts others with similar concerns.

However, if you do not yet have enough clarity to take action, begin by talking with others about your vision. As you do this, your vision may become clearer to you and also to others. It may strike a response in one or two other people. You now have the potential for a community.

Consider the form and size that best suits your purposes. Here you have many choices. We have found creative pairing to be an excellent place to start. Two people, deeply committed to the same task, can accomplish a great deal. On the other hand, as you saw in the last chapter, Beth Burns realized from the beginning that a nonprofit institution backed by a board of directors was her form.

Be aware of the particular ingredients you want to include in your group life. Consider practical parameters, such as time, location, and money. When and how often do you want to meet? Where will you gather? What are the financial considerations and how will they be handled?

✤ Invite Participation ✤

The more clearly you state what you feel called to do, the better the chance you will find collaborators who are similarly called. If you want to invite others to join you, do so in a way that conveys the depth of your interest and also elicits a clear response. Keep these suggestions in mind as you speak about your need for collaboration.

✤ State the purpose and vision of the group you wish to start both clearly and invitingly. Express your own conviction and excitement about what you hope to do.

✤ Describe the connection you see with the broad vision of God. Articulate the particular piece of that vision you feel moved to embody.

✤ Mention the benefits you hope to gain from forming the group, not to "sell" the idea but simply to express why you are pleased to be starting your group effort.

✤ Be specific about how the other person(s) can respond.

✤ Mention the particular ingredients you hope to incorporate in your group life. We have always considered a combination of spiritual nourishment, caring, and task to be essential to healthy and productive communities. If you agree, it is important to state that. Otherwise you may spend much time trying to reach agreement about incorporating those ingredients or being disappointed that they are not included.

✤ Free people *not* to participate. This may elicit a smaller response, but it will be from those who really want to join in your effort. When we feel motivated, it is easy to assume that others will find the same vision or call equally motivating. In reality, only a few usually share the call.

You can share your wish for companions in a variety of ways: spoken in conversation or announced during a gathering or in a longer talk; written in a personal letter; or published in a newsletter. The form you use is less important than your conviction and joy about your new effort.

Local oncologist Jo Magno dreamed of opening a hospice for the terminally ill in our area. Her invitation to participate was given in short talks to area religious and civic gatherings. Beforehand, she had meditated personally on her plan, had sifted it through with friends, and had visited other hospices. In her talks, she shared her personal bouts with cancer, showing within her own life the deep roots of her vision. Giving examples of how the hospice works in Britain, she described how people could be helped to die with dignity, without pain or loss of control, and in surroundings that are personal and attuned to each one's needs.

The response to her specificity and clarity was outstanding. Many people with a wide variety of gifts and representing many segments of society responded with enthusiasm. Excitement peaked when they purchased the attractive Woodlawn School and began converting it into a warm, inviting space for patients and their loved ones.

Billie Johansen, interior designer, heard Jo's invitation and offered her decorating skills to the hospice. Her best attention was lavished on this promising project. When Billie needed help, she issued her own invitation through the local American Society of Interior Designers newsletter for other designers to participate. Her statement is motivating, specific, and personal. Here is a portion of it:

Last week the administrative staff of Hospice of Northern Virginia moved into their new quarters. . . . The project . . . has been gratifying because the planning committee and the people associated with Hospice are so special, and the idea of Hospice is so right and so timely. . . .

It is a project with soul and heart. If I sound enthusiastic—I am. The Woodlawn Design Committee would welcome other designers to a challenge that brings fulfillment. If this sounds fascinating to you, and you would like to join us, give me a call.

Billie Johansen, (phone number)

✤ Organizing and Sustaining ✤

Decide how to incorporate the ingredients you want in the group you form. In the servant community to which we belong, we have divided these into three categories: *spiritual, personal,* and *task.* To address all three yet keep meetings fairly short, our community has activities both within and outside the meetings.

Spiritual: At each meeting we devote some time to spiritual growth or time spent with God. We're also tied together through agreed-upon nourishing activities outside our gatherings, such as studying the same book, grounding ourselves in the common Sunday readings used in churches, and praying using silence, movement, art, or journal writing.

Personal: "Speak about a personal joy and a societal joy." "Share an achievement and a disappointment about work." "What is a way you have kept Christmas this season?" We use invitations like these for hearing about one another's lives. To support members during the month between our meetings, we put our names and concerns on a prayer calendar which is duplicated and given to each person.

Task: We divide tasks quickly. Frequently working on them in pairs, we give much autonomy to each pair. A minimum of time is spent talking about whether or how to do something. Maximum time is devoted to accomplishing it with as much creativity and originality as we can muster, by working within and outside of the meeting.

We attempt to involve the gifts of each person, especially encouraging the use of those gifts that are just beginning to be discovered. We share leadership, taking turns leading our meetings, and also assuming different leadership tasks within them.[4]

We are specific about the time and length of meetings. If we will be late or absent, we tell someone. Regular on-time attendance is not too much to expect of each person. When that erodes, group morale declines.

Gradually you will evolve your own style. Perhaps you will want to write a group covenant, a statement about the purpose, procedures, and activities you want to do together. The process of doing that clarifies commitment and provides a solid foundation as you grow and evolve.

Involve the whole person. Design your activities to engage body, mind, and spirit, both left and right brain, introverted and extroverted ways of being. Balance play and work, prayer and action. Be generous in creating rituals that feed your souls.

Design the time you are together. That is, identify the different things you want to do and the amount of time you want to allot to each. Allow a cushion of unplanned time to take care of unexpected items or lengthier discussions. And be flexible, able to change the plan if needed. Do this by general consensus, negotiating with the group for more time or other changes. We have learned to break a two-hour meeting into segments for opening, personal caring, spiritual nourishment, task accomplishment, and closing.[5]

✣ Recognize and Incorporate Change ✣

A vital group changes and evolves. As you recognize changing needs, devise ways to respond. To grow more competent in your task, find the training you need. To deepen your community life, consider going on a retreat. To strengthen your work, you may need to design another form for your life together. For example, the Partners started out as a "mission group," organized for a common task. Our purpose was to provide ecumenical faith-building events for individuals and churches centering around the *Doorways* courses. But when the courses were published, and we no longer were needed to facilitate them, we began exploring separate work. Several of us received additional personal training to prepare for work as chaplains, pastoral counselors, spiritual directors, and retreat leaders. Rather than working together in a common mission, we began to work separately but still wanted support from one another for our individual ministries. Gradually our group changed from being a mission group into what we call "a ministry support community," organized to support us in separate ministries.

At certain points, members of your community will leave, and new members will arrive. It is important to ritualize these events. And at some point, you may realize that your community no longer has a reason for being. This is a time to remember your life together, mourn the end, celebrate what has happened, and send one another forth.

The kind of activities we have mentioned above take some training and skill to do well. This training could be offered in a concise format such as an event several hours long. To skip training is to invite problems in creating viable communities.[6]

As you take one step, the next one will become clear. You will make mistakes, but they will be your primary teachers if you bounce back quickly, learn from them, and adjust your course. The process of working in community can be uneven, even messy. Yet there will be delightful surprises. Allow for growing pains and celebrate the serendipities. Keep always before you a picture of what you want to accomplish by banding together.

The communities we form are not ends in themselves, isolating us from others. Rather they train us to realize that our community, in the larger sense, is with all people and with the whole creation. When we learn step-by-step to work creatively with someone in our small group who is quite different from us, we will bring more realism and compassion to our view of the differences we see among countries and leaders.

Well-run communities are enormously satisfying. They support us through the ups and downs of life, strengthen our relationship with God, and help us offer our gifts and vision creatively and effectively. In a changing society, they anchor us in the deeper values of commitment, vocation, and solidarity that are what our faith is all about.

GROUP DESIGN

Purpose: To prepare for and run a simulated first meeting of people who have responded to a common call and want to develop a servant community based on that call.

Materials: Newsprint, marking pens.

Necessary Preparation: Two members of the group agree ahead of time to think about and prepare to articulate a call to ministry that has particular relevance for this group. Others in the group can help with suggestions, but the two ultimately must decide on what particular call to issue and how to articulate it in as clear and appealing a way as possible. This group design is most effective when the call is really on the minds of some of the people involved. Therefore, it is hard to give more specific help other than listing some of the calls given in our groups. The situations that these calls addressed include:

- ✚ how to stop pollution;

- ✚ how to welcome and integrate newcomers into our congregation;

- ✚ how to minister to and with the elderly in our area;

- ✚ how to foster world peace;

- ✚ how to nurture and encourage the spiritual life in our parish.

A. Gathering Time, Large Group (*ten minutes*)

Gather the group in a way that is appropriate for you. Consider going around the circle and speaking about one aspect of the Session 5 text that caught your interest.

B. The Servant Community Lab

Because this lab takes up almost the whole session, it is suggested that any small-group discussion of individual work be eliminated unless you choose to budget an extra half hour for that purpose.

1. The Call, Large Group (ten minutes)

The pair who have prepared in advance issue the call. Tell those in the group how they are related to the simulation. For example:

> ✤ "You are the congregation of our church on a Sunday morning, and we are making an announcement."
>
> ✤ "You are the Social Action Committee of the church, and we have asked for a few minutes to speak with you."
>
> ✤ "You are an informal group in our living room, and we are sharing our dream with you."

After you have given the setting, articulate the call in a way that is most appropriate for that setting. Here is an example of a call that was issued in one of our groups:

> I'm concerned about the growing number of Central American and East Asian refugees in our community. Many are having a hard time learning English, obtaining good jobs, and finding places to live. And when they do attain a certain level of success, I find they threaten the longtime residents who are having a hard time keeping good jobs and making rental or mortgage payments.
>
> Jesus taught about reconciliation. I'm excited about the prospects of making that come alive right in our midst. I believe we have a lot to offer these refugees, but they can broaden our horizons as well.
>
> If you'd like to join me in thinking about how we could work with the refugees and residents for the benefit of each group, please see me after church so we can plan a time to meet together.

2.   Group Instructions, Large Group (ten minutes)
Read these instructions or say them in your own words.

"In this simulation, each of you in the room is asked to pretend that the call just issued really grips you personally, and you want to respond. Each of you is asked to join one of three subgroups devoted to a specific dimension of the life of the new servant community that is being formed: spiritual nourishment, support, and ministry.

"Who feels most drawn to working on the task that this group will be tackling? Your job will be to develop ways to study the situation and eventually to do something about it. Please go to one corner of the room to form the *task subgroup*.

"Who is concerned and willing to develop the spiritual dimension of this group's life, to work on how to keep the inspiration going, and to see how it can be nurtured through prayer, Scripture, or other resources? You are asked to go to another corner to form the *spiritual nourishment subgroup*.

"Those who want to help the members of the new servant community to know and care about one another personally, form the *support subgroup* in another corner of the room."

Each subgroup will have thirty minutes by itself to prepare its part of a simulated first meeting of the budding servant community. After the preparation time, the whole group will come together again for the actual meeting, which will be about forty-five minutes long. This allows fifteen minutes for each subgroup to lead the larger group in an activity designed to begin a life together of mutual support, prayer, and ministry.

Allow for some discussion as each one moves into a subgroup. If the numbers in each are badly out of balance, do some trading to assure that there are at least two people in each subgroup.

3. Subgroup Preparation Time, Subgroups (thirty minutes)
    Each group begin by reading the following instructions for
your role in the simulated meeting to come:

a. *Instructions for the support subgroup:* You are to prepare
    and then lead the larger group in fifteen minutes of
    activity that will involve everyone and begin to build
    community. Building community means to help group
    members to know one another, keep in touch with
    what is happening in one another's life, care about
    one another, and share thoughts and feelings about
    the life and work of the group and the individuals in
    it. Naturally, this is a broad, long-range description.
    For your fifteen-minute segment, be prepared to initi-
    ate caring within the group. You might begin by in-
    cluding an exercise that helps people know one
    another in a specific way, for example, sharing feel-
    ings and thoughts regarding the call to which you
    have responded.

b. *Instructions for the spiritual nourishment subgroup:* You
    are to prepare and then lead the larger group in fif-
    teen minutes of activity that will involve everyone
    and provide spiritual nourishment for the group. Spir-
    itual nourishment, broadly seen, includes receiving
    God's love, inspiration, energy, direction, and vision
    for the group's life and work. This can be done
    through Scripture, journaling, prayer, song, nonverbal
    exercises, and so on. For this particular meeting, you
    are to initiate the group in receiving some spiritual
    nourishment related to the opening stages of its life
    and work.

    c. *Instructions for the task subgroup:* You are to prepare
and then lead the larger group in fifteen minutes of
activity that will involve everyone and begin to address the ministry of the group together. Over the
long range, your subgroup will help the whole group
define the task more specifically, identify resources
to help solve the problems involved, and find ways
to carry out the ministry. In your preparation time,
we suggest you use about fifteen minutes to brain-
storm briefly on ways to do the above. Be prepared
to give the large group a five-minute summary of
your own brainstorming, and then use ten minutes
to guide everyone in the larger group in offering
ideas and energy for tackling the task. Your job as
ministry subgroup is not to do the task entirely by
yourself but to guide the whole group in tackling it
together.

    4.   Simulated First Meeting of the Servant Community,
Large Group (forty-five minutes)

    One of the leaders call the group together, remind each
subgroup of its fifteen-minute time limit, and then invite each
subgroup in turn to lead the group for its segment. We find the
best order is: support, spiritual nourishment, task. But feel free to
proceed in another order if that suits the group.

C. Closing, Large Group *(ten minutes)*

    Choose one or two of the following suggestions: evaluation of
session, discussion of details for next session, song and/or prayer. If
you have time, an evaluation can be particularly helpful here.

Speak about what went well, what could be improved, implications for other situations.

Note: This design may seem a bit complicated at first. Also you are creating an "artificial" situation in simulating a first meeting. However, we find that when people freely enter into an experience like this, they can design a simulated meeting that has reality, aliveness, and power. The time limits may seem constraining: You have to move right along or you cannot finish in the allotted time. But this pressure can create a lively, fun atmosphere where some real creativity can occur. Enjoy yourselves and see what happens!

INDIVIDUAL WORK

Purpose: To reflect on the corporate dimensions of your calling.

1. There are many biblical descriptions of how a servant community lives and works. (For example, see Acts 4, Rom. 12, and Phil. 2). Use one of these or another selection to work with this week. What would you like to incorporate into your own life from these descriptions?

2. Review Session 5 and do some journaling on the following questions:

> ✣ Where am I, and where would I like to be as far as call is concerned?

> ✣ Do I feel supported in my call? How? Do I need more support? What would that look like?

3. Evaluate an existing area of service in the light of the three dimensions of Christian life (support, spiritual nourishment, and task).

✤ Are you offering this service more because you feel called, or because you feel you ought to do it?

✤ Is there a balance of support, nourishment, and task?

✤ Are there adjustments of time and emphasis that you would like to make? For example, "I'd like more time devoted to spiritual nourishment in our parish board meetings, not simply an opening prayer."

4.   In light of these reflections, consider taking one concrete step regarding your own area of service this week, and share this with your patron. For example, "I'll bring this up at the next board meeting to see what we can come up with."

5.   For additional ideas on how to begin a servant community, read the following section, "Forming a Servant Community." If you feel moved to organize such a group, consider journaling on the points raised in that section.

6.   Summarize in writing what you did with this assignment.

✤ Forming a Servant Community ✤

You think you have a call. You need others to join in it. You issue the call in conversation, in writing, or perhaps before a wider audience.

Then what do you do with the people who are drawn by the call? Here are some suggested next steps to think about.

1.   *Get the non-negotiables out on the table.* These are the dimensions of the group's life and work that are essential for you. Perhaps you mentioned them when you shared your call. But now share them again because they are crucial for the vitality of the group. For example, it may be essential for you to build regular prayer into the group life, or to meet only at a certain time, or to

be committed to multicultural membership. It is better to start with fewer people who agree on the essentials than to include a larger number who disagree or are unclear about the non-negotiables.

2. *Begin right away to discern, evoke, and organize around the gifts of each member.* This is a never-ending, always changing, and infinitely rewarding process. When a gift is confirmed by the group members, go ahead and use it wholeheartedly. Don't wait for each one to be sure of his or her gifts. That day may be long in coming. But remember that your group works at less than full capacity when any of you is not using your gift.

3. *Gradually reorder your lives to make room for the new priority of your call.* Realize that people do this at different rates, which can cause tension. Understanding needs to balance eagerness as you embark on the demanding task of deepening your awareness of God's love and offering that to others.

4. *Submit plans and communicate developments to the larger community for confirmation.* Approach the decision-making bodies of the larger community for their input, encouragement, and ratification. Stay in communication with them. But don't devote too much time and energy to this process. Constant checking and control drains energy. Take seriously the response of the larger community. If there is resistance, look into and address the reasons for it. If there is enthusiasm, be grateful.

SESSION 6

How Can the Larger Community
Support the Callings of Its Members?

If you have used this book as a course with others, you have learned a common vocabulary and acquired a body of experience that you can continue to use to foster one another's call and gifts. This will likely occur informally as you see one another after the end of the course.

It is also possible to do this more intentionally in the larger communities to which you belong—your church, school, or workplace. This is the focus of this chapter: how do we create larger communities that truly evoke and support the gifts and calling of each one of us? This chapter focuses on how this can occur in the local church, but the ideas are useful in other settings as well.

The question just posed is not new. In the many times it has been asked, the answer that emerges is a grocery list of twenty or thirty ways to foster peoples' vocations: hold retreats, give classes, offer spiritual guidance, provide excellent reading material, share stories of people who are called, visit people at their places of work. Presented with such a list, it is easy to feel overwhelmed.

This is what happened to us when we asked this question. What we did, therefore, was to condense the list into four fountainhead activities that could give birth to the supportive communal culture we believe to be so important. By this we mean the understandings, practices, and processes needed to encourage each person's calling. The four fountainhead activities are spiritual formation and training, servant communities, visioning, gifts and call development.

Recently Archbishop of Canterbury George Carey spoke in Washington, D.C., on the vocations of the whole people of God. What is required, he said, is that the church turn itself inside out. Yes, we should invite people to come into the church. But our primary focus should be on encouraging those who come to move out again bringing compassion and justice to everything they do. The fountainhead activities just mentioned could turn churches inside out. They are meant to support the calls of all church members, whether these are lived within the parish or beyond, as choir directors and Sunday School teachers, or as plumbers, bus drivers, and city council members.

From these "fountainhead" activities, many other developments can flow.

✣ Spiritual Formation and Training ✣

The purpose of most church growth events and courses is to enable people to nurture a life-giving relationship with God. Each offering in itself might be superb. What is often missing, however, is an integrated approach, and an intentional learning track that enables people to develop faith, discern call, and acquire skills to carry that out.

In the churches where we have offered events, we heard people say, "We feel as if we're always in spiritual kindergarten. We never seem to be moving anywhere or being trained to do or be something different."

What we propose is a consciously designed set of activities and understandings that help people move in their spiritual journey and develop increased skills and capacity to be God's people and to carry out their call. This could include several ingredients.

Basic formation in spiritual nourishment, community building, and development of gifts and call. Features we have found crucial in effective training are: leaders who really want to facilitate growth; support people motivated to look after participants and support them through prayer; offerings that combine cognitive content and experiential approaches; and training that fosters movement in participants as they grow from inquirers to committed sharers of God's love.

Such formation can be offered in courses and workshops. But in these days when work commitments seem to take more time and energy, we have to be imaginative in scheduling events in manageable time frames. In considering this, Shelly Wagoner, one of our students, suggested that a local church could select a theme per month and then use every channel available to educate on that topic. For example, if this month's theme is "How to Identify and Use Your Gifts More Fully," then the church newsletter could feature articles on this; a bulletin insert could be available at worship and also sent as mailings; the worship services could be built around the theme; Christian education classes could offer family activities related to it; and meetings could include brief gift-identification experiences. Sherry's aim in this plan was something we all can think about: how to use existing activities for spiritual formation in a way that has cohesion and interconnectedness among the parts. Undaunted by the common complaint "We planned a great course and no one came," she used a variety of means to reach busy people whether or not they could attend a particular course.

Individual spiritual guidance for those who wish companionship and reinforcement by someone called and trained to do this. Many people still do not know that this ministry even exists but are pleased to learn about it. In the congregations we have known, there have usually been people willing to act in this capacity and ready to be trained for it.

Books, pamphlets, and articles on a whole host of subjects—workplace issues, parenting, environmental concerns, bereavement—that are

displayed where readily seen and easily accessible. This is especially
helpful for those who want to learn quietly on their own. In addition, reading an article or book in common can be an excellent
way to build the community as a whole. Ideas can be explored together, new learnings taken further or embodied in group activities.

*Retreats where people can take time apart without interruption to
listen to God and to reflect on their lives.* These initially could be
short events held in the church. Gradually people can be encouraged to attend longer retreats away from home. In most areas
there are spiritual centers staffed by people who are delighted to
offer retreats. The local congregation does not really need to go to
extra work to provide retreats but simply needs to make known
when they are available. Not only are they a wonderful respite for
individuals, but also for groups. When a group attends together,
they often come away with a deeper sense of shared spiritual depth
that is not possible to experience in the overprogrammed life of
the typical church communty.

✤ Servant Communities ✤

As mentioned in the last chapter, there needs to be a variety
of structures for those of us who wish to covenant together to support one another in our callings.

Mike Young, Sonya Dyer, and Carol Dragoo joined with others in a group called "Hope and a Home," dedicated to developing
low-cost housing for disadvantaged people in the District of
Columbia. They are in a mission group because they are on mission together, working on a common task.

No less committed were two young mothers who decided to
study the difficult writings of Teilhard de Chardin while doing the
laundry together in their apartment when the machines whirred.
That way of living the covenant suited their stage in life.

Churches make a mistake when they lift up one type of small group, no matter how worthy, as *the* way to be a church together. What is needed is careful attention to each person's calling to grow and serve, taking into account life circumstance, then helping each one find an effective structure for it, if he or she wants that. So, in any one church, there might be groups for cancer support, affordable housing, occupational support, or worship planning. People can be encouraged to join these or to form others that are more suitable for their situations.

Members of existing groups and church committees may vary in whether they want personal support and spiritual development to be combined with the tasks of their group. Not every group in a church needs to combine those elements. People can be free to operate in this style or to choose another.

✤ Visioning ✤

The familiar verse "Where there is no vision, the people perish" poses a real challenge. How do we open ourselves to God's vision for our congregation in this period of its life? And who articulates this vision? Is it just the pastor or leaders? Or can and should each member have a share in shaping it?

A compelling vision serves as a rudder to steer the ship, seeds the atmosphere with purpose, and provides momentum. When everyone has a hand in forging the vision, each has ownership of what goes on.

Business writer Marvin R. Weisbord suggests how this can be done. Get "everyone into the room," he counsels companies— janitors, bureau chiefs, clerks, and top executives. Remember key moments in company development. Then imagine together "where we want to be ten years from now." Finally, flesh out steps that can move everyone to that future.[1]

When congregations or any institutions engage in such "futuring," people's imaginations are ignited. Everyone is involved. Each person's input is valued.

We encourage you to design a "Festival of the Future" for your church. Here are a few ideas. First, spend time recalling cherished memories, perhaps with objects that symbolize such memories. Then share dreams in response to wonderfully evocative questions such as: "God, what do you want us to be as a people ten years from now? What would our church look like if we were fully attentive to your calling to love and justice?" Draw your dreams on large sheets of paper and share them. Talk through any dreams that need clarification. Finally, ritualize your openness to the dreams and actions you have created.[2]

A common vision forged by the whole church roots the congregation in its unique identity and stimulates its deepening response to the Spirit.

✤ Gifts and Call Development ✤

Encouraging the development of each person's gifts and call is important, and it deserves particular attention. Identify this as a separate function distinct from that of the nominating committee which fills positions needed by the church institution. Then find those who feel motivated to carry this out and give them encouragement to do so. This might be one or more people.

Their purpose would be to help members develop their call to be God's people in business, education, plumbing, printing, homemaking, and all the places they spend their days. The focus would be on developing individuals, no matter where their call leads them.

If you are moved to carry out this function, search for others who feel a similar call. Form a small servant community. Have some fun and name your group. One called itself Isaiah 58. Read that chapter and you'll see why.

Find people who would like support for their commitment to be people of faith at work. Speak with them about what would strengthen their ability to be compassionate and just in the places where they spend each day. For many people, the chance to speak with an interested listener helps them figure out how to meet the challenges they face.

In addition to supporting individuals, you might want to encourage your church to foster each person's gifts and call. Here are two ways to do this that may stimulate your thinking.

Support, recognition, and blessing given either in conversation or during liturgies takes little time but can make a big difference. Biblical people often blessed one another. Why don't we do it? Short appropriate ceremonies, a word or letter of support, public prayer over a person—these are some forms this can take. Praying for different occupational groups and asking them beforehand what they would like to pray for can be deeply reinforcing.[3]

Worship services and liturgies can be occasions to ritualize and celebrate members' gifts and call. Stories of the struggle to be faithful to call, invitations to participate in a common venture, prayers of blessing or thanks for ventures begun or completed—all can be part of worship.

Seed money for peoples' training and projects: One church has established a Cutting Edge Fund. This enabled one member to go to New Mexico for a week of discernment in a desert retreat. Another was helped in adopting a handicapped child. By granting this money for its members' development, the church as a body is saying, "We believe in you. We believe that your searching is important," or "By adopting this baby, you reach out on behalf of us all." Financial support can be critically important to people embarking on something new or untried.

You do not necessarily have to organize these activities your-selves unless you feel inspired to do so. Simply by believing in their value and speaking about them when appropriate, you call forth others who may be motivated to carry them out.

Hindering the Spirit.   There are behaviors that hinder the creative Spirit among people, that foster attitudes of discour-agement, resentment, or fear of trying anything different. Every-one in the church can notice these behaviors and turn them around.

Squelching: The unanswered phone call, the interrupted con-versation that is not resumed—these are little ways the budding sprouts of an idea are killed through lack of encouragement, lis-tening, blessing.

One participant in our courses sparkled when he learned about call. Said another to him, "It sounds as if you're thinking about something wonderful. What is it?"

"I am," he replied. "I've always wanted to establish a listening and caring ministry in our local hospital emergency room."

"Why don't you do it?" he was asked.

"Well, I told one of our church leaders about it, and received such a ho-hum response that I dropped it."

Here was a capable man who could have established this min-istry on his own. All he wanted was a word of encouragement that would have taken five minutes of time and no further involve-ment. When he sensed a lack of interest, his own enthusiasm was squelched for a long time.

Overcontrol: Some churches take so much time making sure everything is cleared, coordinated, and controlled that people are exhausted before they begin. Communication and official blessing are important, but frequently they can be accomplished without the red tape so often involved.

Instead of saying to two people, "Run with the ball," we appoint a committee of ten that cannot find time to meet or that has so many absentees that action is delayed.

Mistrust: Parishes sometimes require more assurance of success for a project than business does. Businesspeople talk about risks and seizing the moment. What a wonderful attitude for the church to take—to trust the inspiration of members and to support their ingenuity in carrying out projects they believe in.

Resistance to Change: When teaching in a seminary, we asked students what attitude most blocks the flourishing of members' gifts and callings. "We've never done it that way before" was the resounding reply.

It is all too easy to think that the new way is wrong. If people who cherish certain traditions can be assured that their ways will not be destroyed, they are more likely to welcome ideas that are different. There is room in churches both for traditional and new ways of offering our gifts to others. No one way is right for all. New efforts can flourish side-by-side with existing activities. Both can be valued as parts of a greater whole.

But this takes attention. We can create an atmosphere that encourages people to share dreams as well as memories, to offer unusual gifts and to use familiar ones, to forge new projects while valuing those that now exist. How wonderful if churches would be places where the traditions are cherished but where the kind of openness suggested by G. B. Shaw is encouraged:

> You see things; and you say, "Why?"
> But I dream things that never were; and I say "Why not?"[4]

In the opening words of *The Prophetic Parish*, Dennis Geaney describes how the local church could play a key role in the renewal of society. Though speaking of the church, his words can apply to other organizations as well.

> This book promotes what may appear to be a ridiculous proposal: that the parish is an ideal place to start a peace and justice movement, not only to renew the local church community, the neighborhood and the city, but to renew the total American and universal church establishment—not to mention local, state, and federal governments and the entire world that is held together by TV satellites.[5]

The idea that the local church can be a seedbed for the renewal of all society is not a pipe dream. It has happened in history and continues to occur now. The black church in the United States is a prime example. Some of the greatest contributors to our culture had their beginnings in local congregations. Maya Angelou, Marian Anderson, Thurgood Marshall, and Andrew Young are a few who come to mind.

The local church is the public face of Christ. It is the place many turn to for spiritual sustenance. When all persons in it know that their gifts are valued and their souls are fed, they form a vibrant body. This is something to work for and pray for and to be grateful for when it happens.

GROUP DESIGN

Purpose: To summarize our learnings from the course and to share where we are in relation to each part of it.

A. Gathering Time, Large Group (*ten minutes*)

Choose a way to gather and settle the group that is appropriate—for example, a song or prayer together, quiet music, or each one briefly stating how you feel about coming to the last session.

B. Sharing Groups, Groups of Four
(*twenty minutes*)

Share the learnings from the individual work that was most important to you. Work out a way to have closure with your small group.

C. Taking Stock and Going On, Individuals
(*thirty minutes*)

1.   Each one look over notes and use about fifteen minutes to respond in writing to these statements:

✦ My strongest gifts are . . . The ones I enjoy using the most are . . . The ones I would like to offer our community are . . .

✦ My experience with patroning is . . . About being a patron I feel . . . About needing a patron I feel . . .

✦ My glimmers of vision are . . .

✦ At this point, my awareness of call is . . .

✦ Regarding the corporate dimension to my calling I have learned . . .

✦ About community, what I would like to offer is . . . What I need from the community is . . .

✦ In summary: How have you grown from this experience? What are the implications for you as you leave the course?

2.   Silent Walk (fifteen minutes)
Take a silent walk through your meeting place. Select an object that symbolizes the growth or challenge you have received through the course.

D. Closing Celebration, Large Group
(thirty minutes)

Devise a way to celebrate the ending of this course. You might like to place a candle in the center of the group. Then one by one each share the object you selected and how it symbolizes what has happened to you in the course.

Another way to end would be to share informally on these topics:

✣ I'm grateful for . . .

✣ I wish that . . .

✣ I'm disappointed about . . .

✣ I learned . . .

✣ What I want to do now is . . .

If there is time, have informal conversation over refreshments.

INDIVIDUAL WORK

(For people who are working by themselves with the course material)

Purpose: To reflect on and celebrate what you discerned through this course.

1. *Integration:* Respond to the questions in C of the Group Design.

Take time to do this prayerfully. You may want to ask for the Spirit's guidance as you do this.

2. *Devise a way to celebrate your discoveries:* Make a collage. Ask for an image of your call and gifts; then depict the image in color and form. Take a walk in the woods and absorb what you have learned. Invite a friend to dinner to share what you learned; ask that person for a blessing for your new awareness.

NEXT STEPS

You have finished reading this book or using it as a course. This has introduced you to questions that can be used over and over to discover your call and gifts in the unfolding circumstances of your life. No one can predict when the answers will come. If you have had some breakthroughs, perhaps you discovered a gift you want to use or a dream you wish to pursue. Celebrate that!

Now you may be asking, "What next?" Here are some options to consider.

Rest: Take some time for the questions and ideas in this book to take root and germinate. If you have used this book with a group, free each person in your group to find their own direction. Don't assume that everyone in the group will want to continue meeting.

Continue with another Doorways *book:* You or your group may feel that this initial *Doorways* experience whet your appetite for more. If that is true, consider using another *Doorways* book as your guide. *Encountering God in the Old Testament* introduces dynamic foundational stories and images that illuminate our calling to be God's people. *Meeting Jesus in the New Testament* enables you to explore the unique gifts God wants to give us through Jesus. It also helps us see how Jesus saw himself as a called person and how to strengthen our view of ourselves as also called.

Journeying with the Spirit offers practice using time-honored tools that have proven effective in opening ourselves more fully to Spirit living.

Lead a new Doorways *group:* If you are one who sees the potential of the *Doorways* books for others, you might want to convene a new group and take the role of facilitator or coordinator. You will continue growing yourself but also enable others to grow.

Pursue your call: You may feel an inner urgency to respond to a particular call. Is this the time for quiet individual development of your call or are you ready to involve others? Don't let anxiety at taking a next step deflect you too much. That is almost always part of creative endeavors. Something new is being born and needs to make way for itself.

Introduce these concepts to your church or another organization to foster people's call and gifts: The suggestions made in this book will help you get off to a good start. As you take concrete steps, you will learn how next to proceed.

Take the insights gained through this book to other arenas of your life: The list of Additional Resources can help you get started.

We are called to sow seeds of grace wherever we are. Alone our contribution may be a drop in the bucket. But combined with others, who knows the effect? Poet/theologian Dorothee Sölle's words to her friends in the peace movement provide a good send-off:

For my young comrades
One plus a friend plus a friend plus a friend
don't say that makes four
the whole is greater than the sum of its parts
small numbers mean friendship
large ones revolution

Begin with what you can count on your fingers
for a friend does not dominate
a friend always has time
or knows someone else who does
a friend always finds an answer

or knows someone else who will
a friend is always competent
or will find someone else who is

Small numbers provide a network
large ones build the new city[1]

ADDITIONAL RESOURCES

The Church of the Saviour's experience with gifts and creativity has been one of our primary teachers. It is well recorded with spiritual exercises and evocative quotations in:

O'Connor, Elizabeth. *Eighth Day of Creation: Gifts and Creativity*. Waco, TX: Word Books, 1971.

To confront pyschic numbing and move to empowering vision, this is a must:

Macy, Joanna. *Despair and Personal Power in the Nuclear Age*. Philadelphia: New Society Publishers, 1983.

A practical, readable global vision for the future:

Brown, Lester. *Saving the Planet: How to Shape an Environmentally Sustainable Global Economy*. New York: W. W. Norton, 1991.

A theological vision for a global renaissance, what it would look like, and the spiritual tools needed:

Fox, Matthew. *Creation Spirituality: Liberating Gifts for the Peoples of the Earth*. San Francisco: HarperSanFrancisco, 1991.

For a readable treatment of Catholic perspectives on discernment:

Green, Thomas H. *Weeds Among the Wheat*. Notre Dame, IN: Ave Maria Press, 1984.

A description of how to discern call in community based on key Catholic and Protestant learnings:

Farnham, Suzanne, *et al*. *Listening Hearts*. Harrisburg, PA: Morehouse Publishing, 1991.

Excellent material on call and ministry, what it is, and steps toward clarity:

> Bonhoeffer, Dietrich. *The Cost of Discipleship*. New York: Macmillan, 1963.
> O'Connor, Elizabeth. *Cry Pain, Cry Hope*. Waco, TX: Word Books, 1987.
> Nouwen, Henri J. M. *In the Name of Jesus*. New York: Crossroad Publishing, 1989.

Step-by-step guide to finding meaningful work either by enriching what you do or finding something new (includes group and individual activities, similar to *Doorways* format; contains spiritual approach to work, but not specifically religious, so it can be used at work as well as in other settings):

> McMakin, Jacqueline (with Sonya Dyer). *Working from the Heart*. San Francisco: HarperSanFrancisco, 1993.

Many useful learnings about living in community at L'Arche by its founder:

> Vanier, Jean. *Community and Growth: Our Pilgrimage Together*. Toronto: Griffin House, 1979.

Three booklets containing more of the authors' ideas on small groups and parishes:

> *New People/New World*. Practical steps to foster prayer service and community in your parish.
> *Parish Small Groups*. Six ways to operate at maximum effectiveness.
> *The Empowering Church*. Communication, leadership, and organizational strategies.

Available from *Doorways*: 1309 Merchant Lane, McLean, VA 22101.

Stages, phases, and patterns of community building:
  Peck, M. Scott. *The Different Drum*. New York: Simon and
    Schuster, 1987.

The biography of the one who most influenced us in our own
community:
  Spink, Kathryn. A *Universal Heart: The Life and Vision of
    Brother Roger of Taizé*. San Francisco: Harper & Row,
    1986.

If you have not used the other books in the *Doorways* Series,
consider:
  Encountering God in the Old Testament. To examine the ques-
    tion "Who is God?" and to experience God as creator,
    caller, deliverer, covenant-maker, suffering servant, and
    new song. This offers a rich foundation for understanding
    the spiritual roots of creativity and call.
  Meeting Jesus in the New Testament. To focus on Jesus' own un-
    derstanding of his vocation and to experience his empow-
    ering of us to extend his compassion and justice.
  Journeying with the Spirit. To experience practices that deepen
    our relationship with the Spirit. These include healing,
    listening, and exploring God's presence over the span of
    our lives.

The *Doorways* Series, when offered in a parish, can be a catalyst
for change in individuals and in the congregation. To learn more
about how a parish can foster the spiritual journeys of members
plus organize to support each one's vision, call, and gifts, inquire
about the authors' "Recreating the Church" packet of articles:
1309 Merchant Lane, McLean, VA 22101.

These organizations have publications and programs that foster our gifts and call:

Cursillo Movement. This Roman Catholic effort offers week-end retreats during which participants are exposed to a rich experience of God's love. There is then opportunity to join reunion groups whose purpose is to keep alive this experience of love and to encourage participants to carry this love to work, home, community, and church. Address: The Cursillo Movement, Center of the National Secretariat, 4500 West Davis Street, P.O. Box 210226, Dallas, TX 75211.

The National Episcopal Cursillo is sponsored by people in the Episcopalian tradition. Address: P.O. Box 213, Cedar Falls, IA 50613. Phone: (319) 266-5323.

The Upper Room Emmaus in Nashville offers a similar experience and is sponsored by Methodists. Address: 1908 Grand Ave., Box 189, Nashville, TN 37202-0189. Phone: (615) 340-7227.

Faith at Work offers training in small group work, shares stories of new models for ministry, and fosters the connection between faith and work. Address: 150 S. Washington St., #204, Falls Church, VA 22046.

National Center for the Laity develops networks of people who search for spirituality that grows out of their daily occupations. Address: I E. Superior St., #311, Chicago, IL 60611.

Laity Empowerment Project is a series of local church-study groups to ignite spiritual lives, gifts, and personal ways of ministering to the world. Address: RRI, Box 29, Adams Center, NY 13606. Phone: (315) 583-5821.

Clergy and Laity Together in Ministry offers training to help people discern their ministries. Address: 5010 Six Forks Road, Raleigh, NC 27609. Phone: (919) 781-5197.

The Center for the Ministry of the Laity emphasizes being God's people in the workplace. Address: 210 Herrick Road, Newton Centre, MA 02159.

Marketplace enables college students to discern and develop their callings. Address: 6400 Schroeder Road, P.O. Box 7895, Madison, WI 53707-7895.

Doorways works with parishes and groups in the areas of spiritual, community, and ministry development. Publication list available. Staff: Rhoda Nary and Jacqueline McMakin. Address: 1309 Merchant Lane, McLean, VA 22101. Phone: (703) 827-0336.

Working from the Heart offers training and publications to help people find meaningful work. Publication list available. Staff: Sonya Dyer and Jacqueline McMakin. Address: 1309 Merchant Lane, McLean, VA 22101. Phone: (703) 827-0336.

The Church of the Saviour offers training and opportunities to visit its various missions. The "Church of the Saviour Guidebook" lists the sister communities, worship schedule, missions, and contact people. It is available from the Church at 2025 Massachusetts Ave., Washington, DC 20036. Phone: (202) 387-1617.

Serendipity House produces written resources and training related to small group ministry. Address: Box 1012, Littleton, CO 80160. Phone: (800) 525-9563.

Christian Vocation Project offers training programs for discerners. Address: 1407 Bolton Street, Baltimore, MD 21217-4202. Phone: (410) 225-9054.

ACKNOWLEDGMENTS

Like all books, this one has a story behind it. Telling that story allows us to thank all the people who helped along the way and also gives you, the reader, some background on how this was written and why.

In a sense this book began when Lois Donnelly, a Catholic, joined with Jackie McMakin and Pat Davis, both Protestants, to offer workshops and courses in local churches. Jean Sweeney and Rhoda Nary, both Catholics, soon joined us. We took the name Partners because we experienced great creativity when as Catholics and Protestants we partnered together to do our work.

Some of us received training in experiential design from Faith at Work. We were inspired by the work of the Taizé Community in France, started by Roger Schutz, a Swiss Reformed pastor, who drew together Roman Catholic and Protestant men to live a monastic life dedicated to "a passion for unity."

Becoming dissatisfied with our "piecemeal" workshops and courses, we were ready for what became a life-changing question: "If you could do anything you wanted in churches, what would it be?"

We had been students at the Church of the Saviour's School of Christian Living and had been deeply affected by the courses offered there. Founded by Gordon and Mary Cosby, its story has been chronicled by Elizabeth O'Connor. Could we design a similar set of courses that would present the treasures of both Catholic and Protestant traditions in a format that busy people could respond to?

What resulted were the four courses contained in the *Doorways* Series. When they were offered, several participants wanted to join us in the Partners Community: Susan Hogan, Cathie

Bates, Dave Scheele, Mid Allen, Ricci Waters, Sally Dowling, Sancy Scheele, Coby Pieterman, and Charlotte Rogers. Each of these people added their ideas to the courses as we developed them further.

Participants then began to ask, "Could you give us the course materials so we could facilitate them ourselves and take them to other places?"

Jackie began to translate the notes and outlines into book form but soon got bogged down. Rhoda volunteered to help, and from then on we worked together, Jackie as writer, Rhoda as editor, both as conceptualizers. The Partners gave tremendous support throughout the process and helped a great deal with finishing touches. Others who helped were Mim Dinndorf, Sonya Dyer, Mary Elizabeth Hunt, Maggie Kalil, Gertrude Kramer, Billie Johansen, Mary Pockman, Janet Rife, Mary Scantlebury, and Gretchen Hannon. Our first editor was Cy Riley from Winston Press.

Liberation, black, creation, and feminist theologies have shown us how limited are our contemporary thought patterns and organizational structures. These theologies stress the Gospel's "preferential option for the poor," the importance of valuing and incorporating the experience of nonwhite, Third World, female, oppressed, and marginalized persons.

In such a theologically fertile period, when new understandings are being lived, shared, and written about at an amazing rate, each choice of word, phrase, or emphasis has theological implications. Whatever we write, in one sense, is quickly dated. Yet, in another sense, we are trying to capture and describe some of the timeless aspects of Christian faith. This book would serve a good purpose if our attempts to preserve the old and incorporate the new stimulated each of you to do this personally.

Since first published in 1984, the *Doorways* Series has found its way to several countries outside our own, most notably Mexico.

There it has enjoyed wide use. A Spanish translation called *Puertas al Encuentro*, including Mexican examples, was created by Mari Carmen Mariscal and associates.[1] Several stories of our Mexican friends are included in this revision.

For this new edition, we are indebted to editor Kandace Hawkinson for seeing the possibility of a brand-new format—each course presented in a single book. She and her fellow editor, Ron Klug, have been wonderful to work with. Others here at home have been a big help, some for the second time: Millie Adams, Marjorie Bankson, Connie Francis, Lynn Parent, Ellen Radday, Gay Bland, Gretchen Hannon, Martha Hlavin, Mary Moore, and Valerie Vesser. Our husbands, Dave McMakin and Bill Nary, and our children, Tom and Peg McMakin and Brendan, Kristin, Kevin, and Paul Nary, have given lots of support, each in different ways.

We would like to hear from you about any reactions and suggestions you have that will help improve this approach to strengthening your spiritual life. If you would like us to partner with you as you consider next steps after using the *Doorways* Series, we are available for consultation, training, and retreats.

Jacqueline McMakin
1309 Merchant Lane
McLean, VA 22101
(703) 827-0336

Rhoda Nary
4820 N. 27th Place
Arlington, VA 22207
(703) 538-6132

NOTES

Introduction

1. For much of the content of this chapter we are indebted to the Church of the Saviour in Washington, D.C. All of our Partners Community attended classes there. The history of this remarkable community is recorded in these books by Elizabeth O'Connor: *Call to Commitment* (New York: Harper & Row, 1963); *Journey Inward, Journey Outward* (New York: Harper & Row, 1968); *Our Many Selves* (New York: Harper & Row, 1971); *Eighth Day of Creation* (Waco, TX: Word Books, 1971); *Search for Silence* (Waco, TX: Word Books, 1972); *The New Community* (New York: Harper & Row, 1976); *Letters to Scattered Pilgrims* (New York: Harper & Row, 1979); *Cry Pain, Cry Hope* (Waco, TX: Word Books, 1987); *Servant Leaders, Servant Structures* (Washington, DC: Servant Leadership School, 1991); and in one by Gordon Cosby, *Handbook for Mission Groups* (Waco, TX: Word Books, 1975).

2. This quotation was found on a greeting card and was not attributed.

Session 1

1. Jonathan Cott, "Forever Jung: An Interview with Marie von Franz." No documentation was visible on this article given to us by a friend.

2. Quoted in the *Dartmouth Alumni Magazine*. No documentation available.

3. Robert Bellah et al., *Habits of the Heart* (Berkeley: University of California Press, 1985), p. 288.

4. Gordon Cosby, *Handbook for Mission Groups* (Waco, TX: Word Books, 1975), p. 74.

5. Gordon Cosby, "Christians and the Love of God," unpublished sermons, Church of the Saviour, 2025 Massachusetts Ave., N.W., Washington, DC 20036, pp. 14, 15.

Session 2

1. Elizabeth O'Connor, *Eighth Day of Creation: Gifts and Creativity* (Waco, TX: Word Books, 1971), p. 34. Here the author defines a patron as "one chosen, named, or honored as a special guardian, protector, supporter, or the like." We are aware of its root word, the Latin *pater,* meaning father, but have not found a better word.

2. Quoted by Ed White in Laynet, vol. 2, no. 3 (Fall 1991), p. 13. *Laynet* is a quarterly newsletter on ministry in daily life. Information is available from Rev. Edward White, 5908 Nevada Ave., N.W., Washington, DC 20015.

3. Alice Walker, "She Smiles Within My Smile," *Sojourners,* December 1986, p. 22.

Session 3

1. Martin Luther King, Jr., *The Words of Martin Luther King: Selected by Coretta Scott King* (Glasgow: William Collins Sons, 1983), p. 95.

2. Walter Brueggemann, *Living Toward a Vision* (Philadelphia: United Church Press, 1976), pp. 15, 16.

3. Inclusive Language Lectionary Committee, *An Inclusive Language Lectionary, Readings For Year B* (Philadelphia: Westminster Press, 1983), p. 138.

4. King, *Words of Martin Luther King*, p. 23.

5. King, *Words of Martin Luther King*, jacket.

6. Worldwatch Institute, 1776 Massachusetts Ave., N.W., Washington, DC 20036.

7. Lester R. Brown, *State of the World, 1992: A Worldwatch Institute Report on Progress Toward a Sustainable Society* (New York: W. W. Norton, 1992). Published yearly.

8. Joanna Macy, *Despair and Personal Power in the Nuclear Age* (Philadelphia: New Society Publishers, 1983).

9. Jacob Needleman, as quoted in Macy, *Despair and Personal Power*, p. 29.

10. Marshall Loeb, "Ideas from a Matchmaker," *Time*, December 17, 1979.

11. Jean Houston, *The Search for the Beloved* (Los Angeles: J. P. Tarcher, 1987), pp. 111–112.

Session 4

1. This material is from telephone interviews with Beth Burns and with Joni Smith, former board chairperson of the Ballet who continues to act as patron for Beth and her work. Beth Burns may be contacted at St. Joseph Ballet, 220 East 4th Street, Suite 207, Santa Ana, CA 92701.

2. Inclusive Language Lectionary Committee, *An Inclusive Language Lectionary, Readings for Year C*, p. 192.

3. This paragraph is a paraphrase of a section entitled "The Way as Conscious Fidelity to 'Inner Vocation,'" included in *The Choice Is Always Ours*, edited by Dorothy Berkley Phillips, Elizabeth Boyden Howes, and Lucille Nixon (Wheaton, IL: Jove Publications, 1948), pp. 61–65.

4. In *Encountering God in the Old Testament*, there is a session on God as Caller, followed by exercises to help you bring your struggles about call to God and to listen for a response.

5. Elinor Burkett, "Builder: We Must Get Our House in Order," *The Miami Herald*, September 4, 1991, quoted in *Ministry of Money* newsletter, December 1991, p. 5.

6. Gerald G. Jampolsky, M.D., describes the seven priciples of attitudinal healing and the work of his center in *Teach Only Love* (New York: Bantam Books, 1983).

7. Frederick Buechner, *Wishful Thinking: A Theological ABC* (New York: Harper & Row, 1973), p. 95.

8. The Giraffe Project, P.O. Box 759, Langley, WA 98260.

9. David Brand, "In Washington: Sticking Your Neck Out," *Time*, August 8, 1988, p. 8.

10. Brand, "In Washington," p. 8.

11. Brand, "In Washington," p. 8.

Session 5

1. Quoted in *The Giraffe Gazette*, vol. 4, no. 4 (Summer/Fall 1988).

2. We are indebted to Lyman Coleman, experienced facilitator of small groups, for this insight. See Additional Resources

section for the address of his community called Serendipity
House.

3. Documentation unavailable.

4. Our article "Everyone's a Leader" gives more details on
   using each person's gifts.

5. Our articles "How to Plan Effective Meetings" and
   "Conducting Prayerful Meetings" offer more details.

6. The four courses in the *Doorways* Series are designed to
   offer this sort of training to equip you to continue growing
   in the life of prayer, community, and calling, either alone or
   in a group. A benefit of the group designs is that they offer
   enough training in group leadership and experiential design
   to continue on your own.

Session 6

1. Marvin R. Weisbord, *Productive Workplaces: Organizing and
   Managing for Dignity, Meaning and Community* (San Francisco: Jossey-Bass, 1987), pp. 281–295.

2. Loughlan Sofield, S.T., and Brenda Hermann, M.S.T.B.,
   Developing the Parish as a Community of Service (Greenwich,
   Connecticut: Le Jacq Publishing, 1984). This describes in
   detail how to create a visioning process and move from there
   to action.

3. This is what Davida Crabtree describes doing in her book
   The Empowering Church (Washington, DC: Alban Institute,
   1989). That is part of the larger story of how one church re-
   organized itself to support member's callings in what they do
   every day.

4. G. B. Shaw, *Back to Methuselah* (Oxford Univ. Press, 1947).

5. Dennis Geaney, *The Prophetic Parish* (Minneapolis: Winston Press, 1983), p. 1.

Next Steps

1. Dorothee Sölle, *Of War and Love* (Maryknoll, NY: Orbis Books, 1983).

Acknowledgments

1. Available from Edamex, Heriberto Frias #1104, Mexico 03100, D. F. Mexico, or from the authors.